PERFECT PICNICS

PERFECT PICNICS

CATHERINE REDINGTON

ILLUSTRATIONS BY
ANTONIA ENTHOVEN

Salem House Publishers
Topsfield, Massachusetts

© Ward Lock Limited 1988

First published in the United States by Salem House
Publishers, 1988, 462 Boston Street, Topsfield,
MA 01983.

Library of Congress Cataloging-in-Publication Data
Redington, Catherine, 1959-
 Perfect picnics.

 1. Outdoor cookery. 2. Picknicking. I. Title.
TX823.R425 1988 641.5'78 87-23579
ISBN 0-88162-354-7

Printed and bound in Spain by Cayfosa, Barcelona.

CONTENTS

INTRODUCTION

Planning a perfect picnic is, in my opinion, as much an art as planning a luncheon or dinner party. The requirements are very similar. At home, you want your guests to enjoy the occasion, so you plan ahead, arranging the setting with lighting and flowers. Table linen is the best you have and the room is arranged to establish a welcoming atmosphere.

You go through your recipes, choosing more sumptuous dishes than you would for an every-day occasion, suited to your guests and the occasion, and select wines to complement the menu.

Everything is planned down to the last detail so that the party goes smoothly and without a hitch. And, at the end, you congratulate yourself on a successful party.

Admittedly, in planning a perfect picnic, you cannot plan good weather also, and in the best-laid plans, nature has a way of getting involved with unexpected winds blowing up from nowhere, or an army of ants deciding to march through the middle of your site. But, assuming that you've taken the precautions of checking weather forecasts and of choosing the venue fairly carefully, a picnic can be as enjoyable, and as glamorous an occasion as any party held in inside surroundings.

For most people, the ideal picnic conjures up an image of a snowy cloth spread under trees with sunlight glinting through the leaves and cool water nearby. Conversation is lazy and relaxed, the food light, appetizing and delicious and a glass of wine helps it down. This is my idea of an ideal picnic also but there are other times of the year, and occasions, that can be just as enjoyable as the perfect summer's afternoon.

The long, summer evenings are, of course, wonderful for picnic entertaining, whether in your own garden or at a special social event such as an open air concert or the theater. Sports occasions, race and boat meetings are also an opportunity for inviting friends to share a special picnic lunch or tea.

Other seasons offer their own particular pleasures: an afternoon's walk in fall could culminate in a delicious, old-fashioned tea or an excursion on a crisp winter's day, such as during the Christmas vacation, might be an opportunity to invite friends to a winter sporting event and you make the occasion special with hot mulled drinks, warming soups or casseroles, and flaky turnovers of meat or chicken, easy to eat and delicious. The early days of spring encourage us to think of venturing on the first picnics of the year, and of course, family parties, especially where there are children, are perfect times for outside entertaining.

The perfect picnic, to me, has three things: first, the food has to be good and varied – as good as you would eat at home, beautifully presented and with all the right accompaniments and garnishes. That is what this book is about – good, if sometimes unusual, picnic dishes for every kind of occasion.

Next, I see no reason why one shouldn't eat from proper plates with knives, forks, spoons and so on, and drink from cups and glasses. For a special occasion, when the bulk of the picnic is no problem, I would take real chinaware and glasses – but there are excellent ranges of attractive plasticware available – and non-breakable 'glasses' also. I like to use a crisply laundered tablecloth and real table napkins, but for a rambling picnic, paper napkins will do, but make sure they are large and thick. Finally, for the perfect picnic, hot food should be hot, and cold food really cold, and you will achieve this happy state with insulated bags and boxes.

Of course, you will not always go to all this trouble for a picnic. There will always be times when you say 'isn't it a great day – let's go out and take a picnic' and on these occasions, you will choose some delicious foods from your kitchen closet and freezer, pre-planned and pre-cooked for just such a time, and it will still turn out to be a perfect picnic.

AT THE WATER'S EDGE

The shore of a lake, or by the sea are tempting places to picnic: the water provides an attractive backdrop and a marvelous playground for the energetic. With the help of watertight bags, rigid containers and ice packs, waterside picnics can be dazzlingly elegant.

Even the keenest swimmer will be tempted out of the water by the thought of an Avocado Swirl or Mushroom Terrine. Serve these as starters with brown bread or Melba toast, or as a main dish with salads. The Poached Salmon and Orange Glazed Ham both make fine centerpieces for the main course. A couple of glasses of refreshing Summer Sparkler should ensure that the afternoon is taken at a pleasantly leisurely pace.

FILO ONION QUICHES

APPETIZER   MAKES 15

10 sheets filo pastry (strudel leaves), thawed if frozen
¼ cup butter, melted
FILLING
1 large onion, peeled and thinly sliced
2 tablespoons butter
¾ cup light cream
1 egg, beaten
2 tablespoons freshly-grated Parmesan cheese
1 tablespoon pine nuts

Lay a sheet of filo pastry on the work surface. Brush it well with melted butter and lay another piece of pastry on top. Continue buttering and layering until you have a stack of 10 buttered sheets. Cut the pastry into 15 squares, dividing the long side by 5 and the shorter side by 3. Working quickly before the butter sets, ease each square into a muffin pan to make a pastry cup.

To make the filling, fry the onion in the butter for 4 minutes until softened but not colored. Divide the onion equally between the pastry cups.

Blend the cream, egg and plenty of freshly-ground black pepper until smooth. Pour over the onion in the cups. Sprinkle each with Parmesan and a few pine nuts. Bake at 400°F for 10 to 15 minutes until set and golden. Cool completely before packing.

CREAMY AVOCADO SWIRL

APPETIZER   SERVES 8-10

1 tablespoon butter
¼ cup all-purpose flour
1 teaspoon dry mustard
¾ cup milk
3 eggs, separated
FILLING
1 avocado, peeled and stoned
2 teaspoons lemon juice
1 teaspoon paprika
½ cup cottage cheese, sieved
½ cup cream cheese, softened
1 tablespoon Parmesan cheese, freshly grated
2 tablespoons thick mayonnaise
freshly-ground white pepper
GARNISH
paprika

Melt the butter in a small pan and stir in the flour and mustard. Cook gently without coloring for 2 minutes. Gradually add the milk and beat well after each addition until a smooth, thick sauce is formed. Remove from the heat and allow to cool for 2 minutes. Beat in the egg yolks.

Beat the egg whites stiffly in a clean bowl. Beat a tablespoon of egg white into the sauce mixture. Fold in the remaining egg white. Spread the mixture evenly into a greased and lined 9 by 12-inch jelly roll pan. Bake at 375°F for 15 to 20 minutes. The swirl will be risen and golden when ready. Turn out on to waxed paper and roll up with the paper. Allow to cool.

To make the filling, mash together all the ingredients until smooth. Season to taste with freshly-ground white pepper. Unroll the swirl, remove the paper and spread generously with the filling. Roll it up again and chill for at least 1 hour before transporting. Pack in a rigid container and cut into slices just before serving.

MUSHROOM TERRINE

APPETIZER   MAKES 6-8

1 small onion, finely chopped
2 cloves garlic, peeled and crushed
¾ cup butter
6 cups mushrooms, roughly chopped
¾ cup red wine
2 bay leaves
2 tablespoons unflavored gelatin
1¼ cups hot white stock
1½ cups cream cheese
2 tablespoons mayonnaise
dash Worcestershire sauce
few drops Tabasco sauce
GARNISH
sliced mushrooms

Fry the onion and garlic in the butter for 5 minutes until softened. Add the mushrooms, wine and bay leaves. Bring the mixture to the boil and simmer until the liquid is reduced by half. Remove the bay leaves. Dissolve the gelatin in the hot stock and add to the mushrooms. Pour the contents of the saucepan into a food processor or blender and work to a purée. Allow to cool slightly then blend in the cream cheese and mayonnaise. Season with freshly-ground black pepper and a dash of Worcestershire sauce and Tabasco sauce. Pour the mixture into a plastic wrap-lined loaf pan. Chill until completely set.

Transport the terrine in the loaf pan. Turn out the mold at the picnic site and peel away the plastic wrap.

SERVING SUGGESTION Garnish with raw mushroom slices and serve with crackers or Melba toast as an appetizer or as a choice of main dish in a meal of several dishes.

POACHED SALMON

MAIN DISH   SERVES 6-8

6 lb piece of salmon or whole sea trout
small bunch of parsley, chopped
¼ cup sweet butter, flaked
¾ cup dry white wine
½ lemon sliced
freshly-ground white pepper
2 tablespoons unflavored gelatin
GARNISH
1 lemon, sliced
¼ cucumber, sliced
water cress

Place the fish in the center of a large piece of foil. Sprinkle over the parsley and flakes of butter. Pour over the wine. Arrange the lemon slices along the fish. Season with freshly-ground white pepper. Bring the edges of the foil together and make a neatly sealed package. Place on a baking sheet and bake at 350°F for 30 minutes or until the fish is opaque when the flesh is parted with a knife tip. Remove from the baking sheet but leave in the foil until cold.

Unwrap the fish and discard the parsley and lemon. Strain the cooking liquor and reserve. Carefully peel the skin away from the flesh and smooth away any dark flesh. Leave the head and tail in position if you are using a whole fish. Lay the fish in a spacious, shallow transportable container.

Make up the fish liquor to 1¼ cups with boiling water. Dissolve the unflavored gelatin in this, heating it a little more to completely dissolve the gelatin if necessary. Cool the gelatin until it thickens a little then spoon it evenly over the fish, retaining some.

Garnish the fish with slices of lemon and cucumber and spoon a little more gelatin over the garnish to keep it fresh. Surround the fish with water cress and chill until required.

For a picnic with several guests, transport the fish whole wrapped in foil. Alternatively, cut individual portions and arrange them on plates, covering the fish with plastic wrap.

ORANGE GLAZED HAM

MAIN DISH   SERVES 6-8

4 lb ham
2¾ cups hard cider
¾ cup orange juice
whole cloves
GLAZE
1 tablespoon clear honey
2 oranges, finely-grated rind only
2 tablespoons light brown sugar
2 tablespoons whole grain mustard

Place the ham in a large pan and cover with cold water. Bring the water to the boil. Remove from the heat and drain the ham. Pour in the cider and orange juice and just enough fresh water to cover the ham. Bring to the boil and then reduce the heat to a simmer. Cover the pan and cook for 1 hour and 5 minutes. Drain the ham and leave until cool enough to handle. Strip off the rind using a small sharp knife, to leave the fat exposed. Score the fat into diamonds and press a clove into the fat at each intersection. Place the ham in a lightly-oiled roasting pan.

Mix together the ingredients for the glaze and spread the mixture evenly over the fat. Bake at 400°F for 35 minutes. Allow to cool completely. To transport, wrap whole in plastic wrap and then foil. Carve at the picnic. Alternatively, carve the ham at home and wrap individual portions. Serve slices with potato salad or ham salad.

ROAST PISTACHIO CHICKEN

MAIN DISH   SERVES 4-6

1 bunch scallions, trimmed and chopped
2 tablespoons butter
1 cup fresh bread crumbs
2 tablespoons fresh parsley, chopped
¼ cup shelled pistachio nuts, coarsely chopped
¾ cup cream cheese
1 egg, beaten
2 cups chicken stock
freshly-ground black pepper
3½ lb roasting chicken
2 tablespoons butter, melted

Fry the scallions in the butter until softened. Stir in the bread crumbs, parsley, nuts, cream cheese and beaten egg. Season with freshly-ground black pepper. Knead with the hands until smooth. Rinse the chicken inside and out and wipe dry with paper toweling. Place the chicken with the neck facing you. Insert your fingers between the flesh and breast skin. Carefully loosen the skin from the breast and thighs. Spread the stuffing evenly under the skin. Reshape the bird with your hands. Place the chicken in a roasting pan. Brush all over with melted butter and pour the stock into the pan. Season with black pepper and cover with foil. Roast at 375°F for 1 hour. Uncover the bird and roast for 30 minutes more. To test if the bird is done, a skewer inserted into the thickest part of the thigh meat should yield clear juices. If the juices are pink, allow a little more cooking time. Allow to cool completely. Wrap in plastic wrap and foil. Carve at the picnic or joint before transporting.

SERVING SUGGESTION   Serve the chicken with a green salad and bread sticks.

CHICKEN CASHEW SALAD

MAIN DISH   SERVES 6

1 tablespoon olive oil
⅓ cup cashews
½ pineapple, peeled, cored and chopped
1 cooked smoked chicken, skinned, the meat torn
into small pieces
1 large avocado, peeled, pitted, sliced into
1 tablespoon lemon juice
2 cups bean sprouts, rinsed
freshly-ground black pepper
DRESSING
2 tablespoons lemon juice
½ cup olive oil
1 teaspoon whole grain mustard
1 teaspoon clear honey
½ cup thick unflavored yogurt

Heat 1 tablespoon of oil in a heavy-based pan. Add the cashews and cook, stirring continuously until they are golden brown. Take care not to over-brown the nuts. Drain them thoroughly on paper toweling and place in a large mixing bowl. Add the pineapple, chicken and avocado and stir in the bean sprouts. Season with freshly-ground black pepper. Turn into a sealed salad container and chill for the journey. The dressing is carried separately.

Place the lemon juice, oil, mustard and honey in a small screw-top jar. Shake until well blended. Just before serving blend in the yogurt. Pour over the salad.

SERVING SUGGESTION A mixed green salad and brown rolls and butter would go well with the dish.

SEAFOOD PASTA SALAD

MAIN DISH   SERVES 4

1 cup uncooked multi-colored pasta shapes
1 cup feta cheese, crumbled or diced
8 crab sticks, or small can of white crab meat, drained
½ cup shelled shrimp
2 scallions, trimmed and finely sliced
½ green bell pepper, cored, deseeded and diced
⅓ cup black olives
TOMATO DRESSING
½ cup olive oil
¼ cup red wine vinegar
1 tablespoon tomato paste
1 teaspoon sugar
pinch dry mustard
½ teaspoon lemon juice
few drops anchovy extract
1 tablespoon fresh parsley, chopped

Cook the pasta shapes in boiling salted water until just tender. Refresh in cold water and drain thoroughly. Place in a large container with the cheese. Cut the crab sticks into chunks (or break canned crab meat into pieces) and add with the shrimp, scallions, bell pepper and olives.

Beat together the ingredients for the dressing until blended. Pour over the salad and chill for at least an hour before transporting.

SERVING SUGGESTION This light salad could be eaten as a main course, followed by cheese or a substantial dessert or cake.

SWEET AND SOUR CARROT SALAD

SERVES 6

2 cups carrots, scrubbed and grated
1 cup root celery, thickly peeled and grated
SWEET AND SOUR DRESSING
6 tablespoons olive oil
1 tablespoon brown sugar
2 tablespoons wine vinegar
1 teaspoon soy sauce
½ teaspoon Worcestershire sauce
1 teaspoon clear honey
freshly-ground black pepper

Mix the grated vegetables together in a container. Beat together the dressing ingredients and add plenty of freshly-ground black pepper. Pour the dressing over the vegetables and toss to coat thoroughly. Chill for one hour before serving.

GERMAN POTATO SALAD

SERVES 6-8

2 lb new potatoes, scrubbed
1½ cups salami or pepperoni sausage, diced
2 tablespoons fresh chopped chives
2 hard-cooked eggs, shelled
6 tablespoons thick mayonnaise
2 tablespoons sour cream
salt, freshly-ground black pepper

Cook the potatoes in their skins in boiling salted water until just tender. Drain and cut in half if they are large. Allow to cool. Place in a container and mix with the salami and chives. Chop the eggs and add to the salad. Blend the mayonnaise and sour cream with salt and freshly-ground black pepper. Mix into the salad and chill before serving.

NEW POTATO SALAD

SERVES 6

1½ lb new potatoes, scrubbed
¼ cup thick mayonnaise
2 tablespoons sour cream
2 tablespoons fresh chopped chives
freshly-ground coriander seeds
2 hard-cooked eggs, shelled, roughly chopped

Cook the potatoes in boiling salted water until just tender. Drain and cool. Combine the mayonnaise, sour cream and chives and season with freshly-ground black pepper and coriander. Pour over the potatoes while they are still just warm. Toss the mixture together.

Turn the salad into the carrying container and sprinkle the eggs over the top. Chill for as long as possible before transporting.

OMELET SALAD

SERVES 4-6

¼ cup butter
6 eggs
½ cup water
salt, freshly-ground white pepper
4 large tomatoes
1 15 oz can artichoke hearts, drained
3 large cooked potatoes
1 tablespoon lemon juice
1 tablespoon fresh chopped basil
1 tablespoon olive oil

Melt half the butter in a 9-inch, heavy-based skillet. Beat half the eggs with half the water and season with salt and freshly-ground white pepper. Pour into the pan when the butter starts to sizzle. Cook over a high flame for a few moments. When set, slip the omelet on to a plate. Cook the remaining eggs in the same way. Roll each omelet up tightly and leave to cool. Meanwhile slice the tomatoes, artichokes and potatoes. Cut the omelet into thin slices. Arrange the ingredients, overlapping in a transportable container. Sprinkle with the lemon juice and basil and seal. Just before serving, sprinkle with the olive oil.

BROWN BREAD ICE CREAM

SERVES 6

1½ cups brown bread crumbs
¾ cups brown sugar
1¼ cups heavy cream
1¼ cups light cream
2 tablespoons thick honey
2 eggs, separated
1 tablespoon rum, optional

Mix the bread crumbs and sugar thoroughly together in a large heavy-based saucepan. Heat the pan gently, stirring continuously until the sugar begins to caramelize. This may take about 10 minutes. When the mixture is crunchy and granular, turn it out of the saucepan to cool on a plate.

Whip the creams together until thick. Beat the honey, egg yolks and rum together. Fold into the cream, followed by the cold crunchy crumbs. Finally, beat the egg whites until stiff and fold into the mixture. Pour into a rigid freezing container and freeze for 2 to 3 hours until the ice cream begins to solidify round the edges of the container. Lightly beat the ice cream with a fork until it is an even texture then freeze until solid.

Spoon the frozen ice cream into a wide-necked thermos to transport it to the picnic.

BRANDY SNAP CURLS

MAKES ABOUT 10

3 tablespoons superfine sugar
¼ cup butter
¼ cup light corn syrup
½ cup all-purpose flour, sifted
½ teaspoon ground ginger
½ teaspoon ground cinnamon
2 teaspoons lemon juice

Place the sugar, butter and syrup in a small saucepan and melt over a gentle heat. Remove from the heat and stir in the flour, ground spices and lemon juice. Drop teaspoons of the mixture, well spaced on baking sheets lined with parchment paper. Bake, one sheet at a time, at 350°F for 8 to 10 minutes until golden brown round the edges but still soft in the center. Quickly remove them from the oven and slide a palette knife under each before draping it over a greased rolling pin. Leave them to cool so that they can form curled shapes.

CREAMY PEAR AND WALNUT PIE

SERVES 6-8

WALNUT PASTRY
2 cups all-purpose flour
½ cup walnuts, finely ground
¼ cup confectioners' sugar, sifted
¼ cup butter
6 teaspoons cold water
FILLING
1¼ cups heavy cream
2 tablespoons white wine
2 tablespoons superfine sugar
2 pears, cored, sliced
1 tablespoon lemon juice
DECORATION
shaved chocolate

To make the pastry, mix the flour, walnuts and confectioners' sugar in a large bowl. Rub in the butter and stir in just enough water to mix to a firm dough. Chill, wrapped in plastic wrap for 30 minutes. Roll out the pastry and use to line a 10-inch pie plate. Line with waxed paper and fill with baking beans. Bake blind at 425°F for 25 minutes. Remove the beans and paper and bake for a further 5 minutes. Allow to cool completely in the plate.

To make the filling, whip the cream until it begins to thicken.

Add the wine and sugar and continue to whip until thick. Spoon into the pie shell. Brush the pears with the lemon juice and arrange on the cream.

Decorate with a sprinkling of shaved chocolate. Chill for one hour. Transport in the plate.

RICH CHOCOLATE SLICE

½ cup, plus 1 tablespoon butter
½ cup superfine sugar
5 eggs, separated
1 cup semisweet chocolate, melted and cooled
¾ cup finely-ground almonds
½ cup self-rising flour
FILLING
¾ cup sweet butter, softened
1 cup semisweet chocolate, melted
1½ cups confectioners' sugar, sifted
DECORATION
confectioners' sugar

Cream together the butter and sugar until very light and fluffy. Beat in the egg yolks then stir in the melted chocolate, ground almonds and flour. Beat the egg whites until stiff and fold into the mixture gently but evenly. Spread the mixture into a greased and lined 9 by 13-inch jelly roll pan. Bake the cake at 350°F for 30 to 35 minutes. Turn the cake out on to a lightly-sugared, clean dish towel and allow to cool completely.

To make the filling, mix together the butter and chocolate. Gradually stir in the confectioners' sugar and beat the filling until smooth. To finish, cut the cake across into three equal pieces. Spread each piece with one-third of the filling. Layer the cake to form a loaf shape. Dust the top of the cake with a little more confectioners' sugar. Chill before packing into a rigid container. Slice just before serving.

HONEY AND PASSION FRUIT MOUSSE

SERVES 4-6

1¾ cups milk
3 eggs, separated
¼ cup thick honey
3 teaspoons unflavored gelatin
6 tablespoons boiling water
1 cup heavy cream, whipped
3 passion fruit

Place the milk, egg yolks and honey in a wide bowl over a pan of simmering water. Cook gently, stirring frequently until the custard is thick enough to coat the back of a wooden spoon. Dissolve the gelatin in the boiling water and add to the custard. Remove from the heat and press a piece of plastic wrap over the surface of the custard to prevent a skin forming. Cool completely then fold in the heavy cream. Cut the passion fruit in half and scoop the edible seeds and flesh from the fruit using a teaspoon. Add to the custard.

Finally, beat the egg whites until stiff and fold into the mousse. Pour into individual dishes or one bowl and chill until set. Serve with a little light cream.

SUMMER SPARKLER

SERVES 6-8

8 maraschino cherries
½ cup cherry brandy
2 teaspoons sugar
1 bottle rosé wine, chilled
¾ cup club soda
DECORATION
4 strawberries

Mix the cherries, brandy and sugar in a small container and seal. Have the wine and club soda well chilled before the journey. Just before serving, mix the wine and club soda with the brandy mixture in a large jug. Float a few sliced strawberries on top.

A WALK IN THE COUNTRY

Exploring the countryside on foot turns an ordinary picnic into an adventure. Walkers are rewarded for their exertions by a wonderful variety of idyllic picnic spots and, once settled, the peace and fresh air make the food taste even better.

Most dishes can easily be carried in a backpack and some of the more manageable snacks could be packed at the top for eating along the way – like the Pork and Cranberry Samosas and Garlic Tortilla in Pita Bread, for example.

Pack a fair amount of substantial food: if it's a wintry day the Hearty Bean Soup makes a warming surprise and can easily be transported in a wide-necked thermos. Follow with Chicken and Veal Terrine perhaps, or Spiced Meatballs served with a dip.

Cakes and pastries make a good excuse for a stop around mid-afternoon. The mention of Flaky Cheese and Apple Strudel, Apricot and Walnut Slice and Choc-nut Rocks will have most people reaching for their backpacks.

TARAMASALATA

APPETIZER   SERVES 6-8

6 tablespoons milk
4 slices white bread, crusts removed
½ lb jar tarama
I scallion, peeled and finely chopped
6 tablespoons olive oil
½ cup salad oil
I large lemon, juice only

In a blender or food processor, pour the milk over the bread and add to the tarama with the scallion. Work until a smooth paste is formed. While the machine is working, gradually pour in the oils very slowly, followed by the lemon juice. Season with ground white pepper. Pack into individual containers. Serve with black olives and strips of pita bread for dunking.

POTTED STILTON CHEESE

APPETIZER   SERVES 6

6 tablespoons sweet butter
2½ cups Stilton cheese, rind removed, crumbled
2 tablespoons port
⅓ cup walnuts, roughly chopped
¼ teaspoon cayenne pepper

Work 4 tablespoons of the butter into the crumbled Stilton using a wooden spoon. Mix until thoroughly blended. Stir in the port, nuts and cayenne pepper. Taste for seasoning.

Pack the mixture into small terrine pots or paté dishes or, perhaps, small paper cups. Melt the remaining butter, strain it through scalded cheesecloth and pour over the potted Stilton to seal. Allow to cool and set. Serve with crackers and celery.

VARIATION   *Potted Danish Blue*
Make as for the Potted Stilton Cheese but use a blue-veined Danish cheese. Add a pinch of celery seeds to the mixture before potting.

PORK AND CRANBERRY SAMOSAS

APPETIZER   MAKES 12

2 tablespoons butter
1 tablespoon oil
1 onion, peeled and chopped
8 oz pork tenderloin, trimmed and diced
1¼ cups white stock
1 tablespoon Worcestershire sauce
1 cup fresh or frozen and thawed cranberries
12 sheets filo pastry
6 tablespoons butter, melted

Melt the 2 tablespoons of butter in a large pan with the oil and fry the onion for 2 minutes. Add the pork tenderloin and cook for 10 minutes. Add the stock, freshly-ground black pepper and Worcestershire sauce. Cover and simmer for 1 hour. Stir in the cranberries and heat through. Remove from the heat.

Work with one sheet of pastry at a time. Keep the rest damp under a wetted and wrung-out dish towel. Brush one sheet of pastry with the melted butter. Fold the top third, lengthways, down over the center third and the bottom third up over the center. Brush the strip with butter. Place a spoonful of the meat mixture at one end of the strip. Fold the end of the strip over the filling diagonally to make a triangle. Continue folding the pastry over the filling, working your way along the strip to finish with a neat triangular turnover. Brush again with butter and place on a baking sheet. Repeat the process to make 12 turnovers. Bake at 425°F for 15 to 20 minutes until golden. Allow to cool on a wire rack. Pack in a rigid container.

VARIATION   Sagey Pork Turnovers
Make as for the Pork and Cranberry Samosas but instead of cranberries, substitute a large peeled and finely-chopped cooking apple and a tablespoon of fresh chopped sage.

CREAMY MUSHROOM PUFFS

APPETIZER   MAKES 16

¾ cup water
¼ cup butter
½ cup, plus 2 teaspoons all-purpose flour
½ teaspoon dry mustard
2 eggs, beaten
FILLING
2 tablespoons butter
1 clove garlic, peeled and crushed
1 small onion, peeled and chopped
1 tablespoon fresh parsley, chopped
1 cup button mushrooms, chopped
¾ cup cream cheese
2 tablespoons thick unflavored yogurt
pinch cayenne pepper
1 teaspoon lemon juice
GARNISH
paprika

Place the water and butter in a pan. Heat until the butter melts. Bring to the boil and quickly add the flour and mustard. Beat well, over the heat for 1 minute. Allow to cool for a few minutes. Gradually beat in sufficient eggs to form a smooth glossy paste that will just hold its shape. Spoon the mixture into a pastry bag fitted with a large plain nozzle and pipe about 16 small rounds on greased baking sheets. Bake at 425°F for 25 to 30 minutes until very crisp. Cool on a wire rack.

To make the filling, melt the butter in a pan and fry the garlic and onion for 2 minutes. Add the parsley and mushrooms and cook for 5 minutes. Allow to cool. Blend together the cheese, yogurt, pepper and lemon juice in a bowl. Season and stir in the mushroom mixture. Chill.

Just before packing, split the puffs and fill them with the mixture. Dust with a little paprika and pack the puffs into rigid containers.

VEGETABLE STICKS WITH BLUE CHEESE DIP

APPETIZER   SERVES 4-6

DIP
I egg yolk
2 teaspoons white wine vinegar
pinch dry mustard
¾ cup olive oil
2 teaspoons boiling water
I teaspoon lemon juice
½ cup cottage cheese, sieved
½ cup Danish blue cheese, crumbled
TO SERVE
celery, carrots, cucumber and peppers cut into sticks

Place the egg yolk in a bowl with the vinegar, mustard and a little salt and freshly-ground white pepper. Beat together. Gradually beat in the olive oil, drop by drop at first, until it is all absorbed and the mixture is thick and shiny. Beat in the boiling water and lemon juice. Blend the cottage and blue cheeses together and stir evenly through the dip.

Serve in small sealed containers. Wrap the vegetable sticks in plastic wrap and chill well before packing.

FRESH TOMATO CHUTNEY

SERVES 6

6 ripe tomatoes
1 onion, peeled and finely chopped
1 lime, finely-grated rind and juice
2 tablespoons fresh mint or coriander, chopped
few drops Tabasco sauce

Plunge the tomatoes in boiling water for 10 seconds. Drain and peel away the skins. Cut in half and remove the seeds and tough stalk base. Chop the flesh finely. Mix with the remaining ingredients and check the seasoning for salt. Pack into small pots and serve with the terrine.

HEARTY BEAN SOUP

MAIN DISH   SERVES 6

½ cup red kidney beans
½ cup navy beans
½ cup white kidney beans
½ cup pinto beans
1 tablespoon oil
3 slices bacon, derinded, chopped
1 large onion, peeled and chopped
2 sticks celery, chopped
5½ cups stock
1 14 oz can chopped tomatoes
1 teaspoon dried mixed herbs
1 teaspoon Worcestershire sauce
freshly-ground black pepper, salt
¼ cup fresh parsley, chopped

Soak all the beans together in a large bowl of cold water overnight. Drain and rinse thoroughly. Cover with fresh water and simmer for 1 hour.

Heat the oil in a large pan. Fry the bacon, onion and celery for 5 minutes. Drain the beans and add to the pan with the stock, tomatoes, herbs and Worcestershire sauce. Season with freshly-ground black pepper. Do not add salt at this stage as it toughens the beans. Simmer for 1 hour. Add the parsley and season with a little salt if desired. Transport in a wide-necked thermos.

CHICKEN AND VEAL TERRINE

MAIN DISH   SERVES 6-8

1 lb chicken breasts, skinned, boned and finely chopped
½ cup cooked long-grain rice
½ teaspoon mixed spice
pinch ground mace
2 tablespoons butter
¾ cup button mushrooms, chopped
2 sticks celery, chopped
1 cup cottage cheese, sieved
¾ cup milk
1 egg white
1 tablespoon lemon juice
freshly-ground white pepper
2 ¼ lb veal scallops
2 bunches water cress, finely chopped
½ cup stuffed green olives, chopped

Place the chicken, rice, spice and mace in a food processor and blend until very smooth. Cover and place in the freezer for 30 minutes. Melt the butter in a skillet and cook the mushrooms and celery for 5 minutes. Drain, cool and put aside. Blend the cottage cheese and milk until smooth. Beat the egg white stiffly and fold in. Gently fold the cheese mixture into the chicken. Stir the lemon juice into the mushroom mixture. Season with freshly-ground white pepper. Place the veal slices between two sheets of plastic wrap and beat out very thinly. Mix together the water cress and olives. Spoon half the chicken mixture into a greased 2 lb loaf pan.

Lay the veal out to make a strip as long as the pan. Place the water cress mixture along one long edge and roll the veal up to make a long tube. Place this down the center of the half-filled pan and carefully spoon the remaining chicken mixture on top. Knock the pan sharply on the work surface to settle the contents. Cover and place in a roasting pan filled with 1-inch boiling water. Bake at 400°F for 1¼ hours. Cool in the pan. Turn out and wrap in plastic wrap and foil before packing and slice before serving. Alternatively, cut slices of terrine before leaving home and wrap individually.

SERVING SUGGESTION Eat the terrine with bread rolls or pita bread and fresh tomato chutney.

GARLIC TORTILLA IN PITA BREAD

MAIN DISH   SERVES 4

¼ cup butter
1-2 cloves garlic, peeled and crushed
1 onion, peeled and sliced
2½ cups cooked potato, diced
⅔ cup cooked ham, chopped
4 eggs
2 teaspoons cold water
salt, freshly-ground black pepper
2 tablespoons fresh parsley, chopped
4 whole wheat pita breads, split and buttered
crisp lettuce

Heat the butter in a deep skillet. Add the garlic and onion and cook for 2 minutes. Add the potato and ham and cook for a further 10 minutes. Beat the eggs with the water and season with salt and ground black pepper. Beat in the parsley. Pour the egg mixture over the vegetables. Allow to cook for 10 to 15 minutes over a low heat until set. Turn out on to a board and allow to cool.

Cut into eight wedges and slip these into the pita bread pockets. Add pieces of crisp lettuce and wrap individually in foil.

Small, ripe tomatoes are good with these.

SPICED MEATBALLS AND DIP

MAIN DISH   SERVES 4-6

¼ cup fresh white bread crumbs
½ lb lean ground beef
1 egg, beaten
½ teaspoon *garam marsala*
½ teaspoon ground allspice
1 teaspoon fresh chives, chopped
1 teaspoon fresh parsley, chopped
oil for shallow frying
DIP
1¼ cup thick unflavored yogurt
¾ cup sieved canned tomatoes
few drops Tabasco sauce
½ teaspoon Worcestershire sauce
2 tablespoons fresh parsley, chopped
salt, freshly-ground black pepper

Mix together the bread crumbs, beef, egg, spices and herbs. Knead with the hands to a smooth mixture. Form into 24 small balls. Cover and chill for 1 hour. Heat the oil and fry the meatballs for 10 minutes, turning occasionally. Drain thoroughly on paper toweling, and pack into small containers with toothpicks for spearing.

To make the dip, blend together all the ingredients and season well with salt and freshly-ground black pepper. Pack into small sealed containers and chill.

PEPPERY CHICKEN TURNOVERS

MAIN DISH   MAKES 6

6 chicken breasts, skinned and boned
¾ cup cream cheese
¾ cup cottage cheese, sieved
1½ tablespoons tomato paste
1 teaspoon pink or green peppercorns, drained
and crushed
1 teaspoon fresh oregano, chopped
few drops Tabasco sauce
1 canned red pimento, drained and finely chopped
12 oz ready-made puff pastry
1 egg, beaten
2 tablespoons sesame seeds

Place the chicken breasts between two sheets of plastic wrap. Beat with a rolling pin to flatten the meat evenly. Beat together the cheeses, tomato paste, peppercorns, oregano and Tabasco. Divide this mixture into six portions and spread evenly over the chicken breasts. Sprinkle the chopped pimento over the filling. Roll each chicken breast up from the pointed end, wrap in plastic wrap and chill for 30 minutes.

Divide the pastry into 6 pieces and roll each piece out thinly to a rectangle 3 times as wide as the chicken rolls. Unwrap the rolls. Brush the edges of the pastry with beaten egg and enclose each chicken roll in pastry. Place on a baking sheet with the joins underneath.

Brush the turnovers with beaten egg and slash the pastry with a knife to decorate. Sprinkle with sesame seeds. Bake at 425°F for 25 minutes until golden brown. Allow to cool on a wire rack.

Pack in a rigid container for transporting.

APRICOT BRANDY CREAM MOUSSE

SERVES 4-6

1 tablespoon unflavored gelatin
¼ cup boiling water
2 eggs, separated
3 tablespoons superfine sugar
¼ cup apricot brandy
¾ cup heavy cream

Dissolve the gelatin in boiling water. Place the egg yolks, sugar and brandy in a wide bowl over a pan of simmering water. Beat for 5 to 10 minutes until the mixture is thick and foamy. Beat the dissolved gelatin into the egg and sugar mixture. Remove from the heat and continue to beat until cool.

Whip the cream until thick and fold in. Beat the egg whites stiffly and fold in. Spoon into individual containers and chill until set.

FLAKY CHEESE AND APPLE STRUDEL

MAKES 18 SLICES

This recipe makes about 18 slices but it's not worth making the dough in smaller quantities. Strudel freezes well so it can be stored.

DOUGH
6 tablespoons warm water
1 egg beaten
1 tablespoon butter, melted
1¾ cups all-purpose flour
pinch of salt
FILLING
1 cup cottage cheese, sieved
¾ cup cream cheese, softened
2 egg yolks
1 lemon, finely-grated rind only
1 tablespoon cream of wheat
2 tablespoons hazelnuts, finely ground
¾ cup soft brown sugar
⅓ cup white raisins
½ cup butter, melted
1 cup fresh white bread crumbs
3 cooking apples, peeled, cored and thinly sliced
1 teaspoon ground mixed spice

To make the dough, beat together the water, egg and melted butter. Mix this into the flour and salt to make a dough. Knead well for about 10 minutes until the dough is soft, smooth and elastic. Wrap in plastic wrap and leave to relax for 30 minutes.

To make the filling, beat together the cheeses and egg yolks. Work in the rind, cream of wheat, nuts, sugar and raisins.

Smooth a large clean cloth over the work surface. Dust lightly with flour and roll out the dough on this as thin as you can. Pull the dough very gently with your hands until it is very thin and almost transparent. Trim the edges neatly with scissors. Brush all over with the melted butter and sprinkle with bread crumbs. Spread the cheese mixture and arrange the apple slices on top. Sprinkle with the spice. Roll up the dough from a short side with the help of the cloth. Bend the roll into a horseshoe shape so that it will fit on to a large greased baking sheet.

Bake at 450°F for 10 minutes then reduce the heat to 400°F for a further 20 minutes. Allow to cool. Cut into slices interleaved with waxed paper.

APPLE AND ALMOND DANISH PASTRIES

MAKES 8

2 cups all-purpose flour
pinch of salt
½ cake compressed yeast
½ cup milk, warmed slightly
½ egg
2 tablespoons butter, melted
6 tablespoons butter, chilled
FILLING
3 tablespoons superfine sugar
¼ cup butter
½ cup ground almonds
6 tablespoons apple purée
6 tablespoons apricot jelly, warmed

Sift the flour and salt together into a warmed bowl. Blend the yeast and the milk. Beat in the egg and melted butter.

Add these liquids to the flour and mix to a smooth dough with a wooden spoon. Knead for 10 minutes until the dough is soft, silky and elastic. Leave to rest in the refrigerator in an oiled plastic bag for 15 minutes. Punch the dough to knock out the air and knead once more until smooth. Roll out on a lightly-floured surface to a long rectangle.

Divide the chilled butter in half. Using half the butter, dot small flakes of it over the top two-thirds of the dough. Fold up the bottom third over the center and the top third down on top of them. Press the edges of the dough to seal. Chill for 20 minutes. Give the dough a quarter turn, clockwise. Roll out to the same size as before. Dot with the remaining butter and repeat the process. Chill and repeat the rolling and folding sequence twice more. Leave the dough to rest in the refrigerator for at least 4 hours. Roll out the dough to about ¼-inch thick in a rectangle of 8 by 16 inches. Cut into two rows of 4 squares.

Beat all the ingredients for the filling together until smooth. Place a spoonful of filling on the center of each square. Bring two opposite corners of each square up over the filling and press down to seal. Place the pastries on a greased baking sheet. Allow to rise in a warm place, covered in oiled plastic wrap. Remove the film and bake at 425°F for 10 to 12 minutes. Brush with warm jelly and allow to cool on a wire rack.
Pack into rigid containers.

GINGERED ALMOND LOAF

SERVES 8-10

½ cup butter
½ cup superfine sugar
2 eggs, beaten
1½ cups self-rising flour
½ cup ground almonds
¼ cup stem ginger, chopped
DECORATION
2 tablespoons stem ginger, chopped

Cream the butter and sugar together until light and fluffy. Gradually beat in the eggs, creaming well after each addition. Fold in the flour and almonds and stir in the ginger. Turn into a greased and lined 2 lb loaf pan and sprinkle the remaining stem ginger over the top. Bake at 350°F for 45 to 50 minutes. When a skewer inserted comes out clean the cake is done. Cool in the pan for 10 minutes then turn out on to a wire rack. Pack, cut into slices and buttered if liked.

VARIATION   *Apricot and Walnut slice*
Make as for the Gingered Almond Loaf but substitute 1 cup of chopped dried apricots for the ginger and chopped walnuts for the ground almonds. Decorate with chopped dried apricots.

CHOC-NUT ROCKS

MAKES 12

¼ cup butter
¼ cup light corn syrup
1 5 oz packet chocolate-covered graham crackers,
chopped
¼ cup white raisins
¼ cup walnuts, chopped

Melt the butter and syrup together in a pan over gentle heat. Stir in the remaining ingredients. Turn into a greased, lined 2 lb loaf pan. Press down and chill until set. Turn out and cut into 12 small triangles. Wrap individually in foil and keep as cool as possible before and during transporting.

FRUITED FLAPJACK

12 FINGERS

¾ cup dried apricots
⅓ cup dried peaches
¾ cup dried bananas
⅓ cup white raisins
2 oranges, finely-grated rind and juice
2¾ cups rolled oats
2¼ cups whole wheat flour
¾ cup light brown sugar
¾ cup, plus 2 teaspoons butter
2 tablespoons light corn syrup

Place the dried fruits, orange rind and juice in a pan and bring to the boil. Simmer gently, stirring frequently for 5 minutes until softened. Cool and put aside. Mix the oats and flour in a large bowl. Place the sugar, butter and syrup in a pan and melt together. Pour on to the oats and flour and mix in. Spread half the oats mixture into the base of a greased and lined 7 by 11-inch pie plate. Spread the fruit mixture evenly over this and top with the remaining oat mixture. Press down firmly.

Bake at 375°F for 25 to 30 minutes until golden brown. Mark into fingers and cool in the plate. Turn out and cut up.

Pack, interleaved with waxed paper in a rigid container.

LEMON APRICOT CHEESECAKE

SERVES 4-6

½ lb chocolate-covered graham crackers, crushed
⅓ cup sweet butter
FILLING
I cup cream cheese
½ cup superfine sugar
2 eggs, separated
I lemon, grated rind and juice
small can of apricots in natural juice, drained,
chopped
½ oz gelatin dissolved in 3 tablespoons of boiling
water
¾ cup whipping cream
DECORATION
Strips of lemon peel

Place the cookies in a bowl. Melt the butter and pour over. Mix until evenly blended. Press the mixture into the base of an oiled, loose-based 8-inch cake pan. Chill until set firm.

To make the filling, beat the cheese with the sugar, egg yolks, lemon rind and juice until smooth. Stir in the apricots and cooled gelatin. Whip the cream and fold in. Finally, whip the egg whites stiffly and gently fold in. Pour the filling on to the cookie base and chill until set. Transport in the pan.

Run a knife round the outside of the pan to release the cheesecake. Decorate with lemon strips and serve on the pan's base with half and half cream.

HOMEMADE LEMONADE

SERVES 6-8

I lemon
I teaspoon cream of tartar
1¼ cups sugar

Wash the lemon in hot water to release the oils in the rind.

Thinly pare the rind into a bowl. Add the cream of tartar and the sugar. Pour on just enough boiling water to cover. Stir to dissolve the sugar. Add the juice of the lemon. Allow to stand, covered for 24 hours.

Serve diluted to taste with ice water. Either keep chilled in a thermos or on a hot day try freezing the diluted drink in a plastic bottle not filled quite to the top. Pack the frozen drink and it will have just melted and be ice cool by lunchtime!

SUMMER INTERLUDE

A hot summer's afternoon is best spent outside, in the shade of an overhanging tree, cooled by a light breeze. A picnic lunch is the perfect excuse for this. Choose a spot, open the hamper and prepare for a leisurely afternoon.

With a little invention and patience even the most fragile dishes can be successfully packed and transported. The Seafood Cocktail, which is served cupped in a crisp curl of lettuce, travels well and makes an attractive appetizer.

Cool salads and delicate-flavored fish ideas tantalize the lazy mid-summer appetite. Creamy Apple and Horseradish Chicken with Mixed Wild Rice Salad and Rosemary Bread Sticks could be served to a party of hearty eaters, while tempting snacks like Olive and Anchovy Bread satisfy the whims of casual nibblers. Finish the picnic with chilled Kiwi Citrus Fruit Salad or ice-cold Cassata.

SEAFOOD COCKTAILS

APPETIZER   SERVES 8

1 iceberg lettuce heart
3 sticks celery, thinly sliced
½ cup shelled shrimp
1 cup light and dark crab meat, defrosted if frozen
1 7 oz can tuna fish, drained and flaked
SAUCE
¾ cup mayonnaise
6 tablespoons thick unflavored yogurt
1 tablespoon tomato paste
¾ cup heavy cream, whipped
1 tablespoon lemon juice
few drops Tabasco sauce
few drops Worcestershire sauce
GARNISH
lemon slices
alfalfa sprouts

Separate the lettuce heart carefully into small leaves that curl to form a cup shape. Chill them in a sealed container. Mix the celery, shrimp, crab meat and tuna fish. In another bowl combine the mayonnaise, yogurt, tomato paste, cream, lemon juice, Tabasco and Worcestershire sauce. Season with freshly-ground white pepper. Mix the sauce with the fish and spoon the mixture into the lettuce cups. Pack them close together in a container garnished with the lemon slices and sprouts. Chill before transporting. These are picked up and eaten with the fingers.

TRICOLOR VEGETABLE TERRINE

APPETIZER   SERVES 8

2½ cups carrots, peeled and chopped
1¼ cups potatoes, peeled and chopped
½ cauliflower, cut into florets
1 orange, grated rind and juice
¼ cup Swiss cheese, grated
1 bunch water cress, trimmed and chopped
1 lb package frozen chopped spinach, thawed
4 tablespoons unflavored gelatin
¾ cup boiling chicken stock or water
6 tablespoons mayonnaise
3 egg whites, stiffly beaten

Cook the carrots, potatoes and cauliflower separately in salted boiling water until tender. Drain. Purée the carrots in a blender or food processor with the orange rind and juice. Purée the potatoes and cauliflower with the cheese. Purée the water cress and spinach together. Season each mixture.

Dissolve the gelatin in the stock or water and cool. Divide the dissolved gelatin, mayonnaise and egg white equally between the three purées. Spoon the carrot mixture into the base of a greased and lined 2 lb loaf pan or terrine. Chill in the freezer until set. Spoon the cauliflower purée on top and chill until set. Finally top with the water cress purée and chill in the refrigerator until completely set.

Cover and transport in the terrine. Turn out just before serving and cut into slices. Alternatively, cut the terrine into slices at home and wrap individually.

SERVING SUGGESTION   Greek salad and saffron bread would make a substantial meal with the terrine.

MUSHROOM QUICHE

APPETIZER   SERVES 4-6

PASTRY
¼ cup butter
1 cup self-rising whole wheat flour
1 tablespoon Parmesan cheese, finely grated
1 teaspoon whole grain mustard
2-3 tablespoons iced water
FILLING
¼ cup butter
1 onion, peeled and sliced
1 clove garlic, peeled and crushed
3 cups button mushrooms, sliced
2 eggs, beaten
¾ cup heavy cream
1 teaspoon coriander seeds, freshly ground
½ cup Gruyère cheese, grated

To make the pastry, rub the butter into the flour. Mix in the Parmesan and mustard and just enough water to form a firm dough. Wrap in plastic wrap and chill for 20 minutes. To make the filling, melt the butter in a large shallow pan and fry the onion and garlic for 2 minutes. Add the mushrooms and cook for 5 minutes. Beat together the eggs, cream and coriander. Season with freshly-ground white pepper.

Roll out the pastry on a lightly-floured work surface. Use to line an 8-inch quiche pan or plate. Set on a baking sheet. Spoon the cooked mushroom mixture into the quiche and pour over the eggs. Scatter the cheese over the top and bake at 350°F for 25 to 30 minutes until set and golden brown. Cool and transport in the pan or plate. Cut into slices to serve.

SHRIMP AND ASPARAGUS MOUSSE

APPETIZER   SERVES 6-8

2 12oz cans asparagus spears, drained
½ cup thick unflavored yogurt
6 tablespoons mayonnaise
½ cup cottage cheese, sieved
1 cup cream cheese
4 teaspoons unflavored gelatin
1 tablespoon lemon juice
few drops Tabasco sauce
¼ teaspoon paprika pepper
2 tablespoons fresh parsley, chopped
1 cup cooked, shelled shrimp

Place the asparagus, yogurt, mayonnaise and cheeses in a blender or food processor. Blend to a smooth purée. Sprinkle the gelatin over the boiling water in a small bowl and stir until dissolved. Cool. Add to the asparagus cream with the lemon juice, Tabasco, paprika and parsley. Season with freshly-ground white pepper. Stir in the shrimp and pour into a container for transporting. Chill until set. Serve in scoops with salad.

SALMON AND LEMON TERRINE

MAIN DISH   SERVES 8-10

1 lb fillets of flounder, skinned and cut into pieces
¾ cup fresh white bread crumbs
2 lemons, grated rind of both, juice of one
½ cup dry white wine
¾ cup light cream
2 tablespoons butter
2 tablespoons fresh dill, chopped
2 tablespoons fresh parsley, chopped
1 tablespoon fresh chives, chopped
½ lb strip fresh salmon fillet

Place the flounder, bread crumbs, lemon rind and juice, wine and cream in a food processor and work until quite smooth. Season with freshly-ground white pepper. Chill for 1 hour. Thoroughly coat the inside of a 2 lb loaf pan or terrine with the butter. Place the herbs in the pan and tip the pan in all directions to coat the sides and base completely with herbs.

Spoon half the fish purée into the prepared pan and lay the piece of salmon along it. Spoon in the remaining fish purée and smooth the top. Tap the pan on the work surface to settle the contents.

Cover and stand in a roasting pan half filled with boiling water. Bake at 400°F for 1 hour. Cool and transport in the pan. Serve in slices. Alternatively, the terrine can be cut into slices before leaving home and individually wrapped.

SERVING SUGGESTION Serve the terrine with New Potato Salad (page 16) and coleslaw.

CREAMY APPLE AND HORSERADISH CHICKEN

MAIN DISH   SERVES 6-8

1 stewing chicken (approximately 3½ lb)
bouquet garni
2 cooking apples, peeled, cored and sliced
1¼ cups mayonnaise
2-3 teaspoons fresh horseradish, grated
¾ cup whipping cream, whipped

Wash the bird inside and out. Place in a large pan with the bouquet garni and cover with cold water. Cover, bring to the boil and simmer for about 1 hour, or until tender. Reserve a little of the stock and drain the bird. Allow to cool. Remove and discard the skin and bones and cut the flesh into bite-sized pieces.

Place the apples in a pan with 2 tablespoons of the reserved stock and simmer until reduced to a thick purée. Cool. Stir into the mayonnaise with the horseradish and whipped cream. Stir in the chicken and chill before serving. Transport the chicken in a shallow container and keep as cool as possible.

RAISED CHICKEN AND HAM PIE

MAIN DISH   SERVES 8-10

6 cups all-purpose flour
2 teaspoons salt
½ cup shortening
¼ cup butter
1¼ cups water
FILLING
1 lb cooked chicken, skin and bones removed
1 lb cooked ham, rind removed
1 onion, peeled and chopped
¼ cup mild whole grain mustard
½ teaspoon ground mace
1 egg, beaten
2 teaspoons unflavored gelatin
1¼ cups boiling chicken stock
¼ cup fresh parsley, chopped

Sift the flour and salt into a mixing bowl and make a well in the center. Place the shortening, butter and water in a small pan. Heat until melted then bring to the boil. Pour into the flour and quickly mix to a fairly soft dough. Turn out on to a lightly-floured work surface and knead until smooth.

Reserve one quarter of the pastry and put aside, covered in a warm place. Use the remaining pastry to line the base and sides of a large raised pie mold. Slice the chicken and ham and layer this into the lined mold, scattering the layers with the onion, mustard and mace. Season with salt and freshly-ground black pepper. Roll out the reserved pastry and use to make a lid and cover the pie. Dampen the edges to seal. Trim, crimp the crusts and decorate with the trimmings. Cut a small hole the size of a penny in the center of the lid. Brush the lid and decorations with beaten egg. Bake at 400°F for 30 minutes. Brush again with beaten egg and reduce the oven temperature to 325°F for 45 minutes until golden brown. Dissolve the gelatin in the stock, check the seasoning and stir in the parsley. As the pie cools, pour in the stock through the hole in the lid using a small funnel. Chill overnight.

Transport the pie in the pan. Serve in slices with salad.

MIXED WILD RICE SALAD

SERVES 6-8

¼ cup wild rice
½ cup long-grain rice
1 red bell pepper, cored, deseeded and diced
1 cup canned corn, drained
1 cup cooked green beans
DRESSING
2 tablespoons lemon juice
6 tablespoons olive oil
2 tablespoons fresh parsley, chopped
2 tablespoons fresh chives, chopped
pinch of sugar
pinch of ground mace
1 teaspoon whole grain mustard

Pour boiling water over the wild rice to cover. Leave standing for 2 to 3 minutes. Drain. Cook the long-grain rice in plenty of boiling salted water until tender – about 12 minutes. Drain and rinse in cold water. Mix the two rices then mix in the pepper, corn and beans. Place all the dressing ingredients in a small screw-top jar and shake together until well blended. Add freshly-ground black pepper and pour over the rice. Toss to coat.
Transport the salad in a sealed container.

SALAD NIÇOISE

SERVES 6-8

¾ cup green beans, cooked until tender
2 large potatoes, peeled and cooked and cut into pieces
4 hard-cooked eggs, shelled and cut into wedges
4 ripe tomatoes, chopped
¼ cup black olives
1 14 oz can tuna fish, drained
½ oz anchovies, drained
DRESSING
¼ cup olive oil
1 tablespoon white wine vinegar
pinch of sugar
pinch of salt
pinch of dry mustard
¼ teaspoon dried mixed herbs
1 teaspoon lemon juice

Combine the beans, potatoes, eggs, tomatoes, olives and tuna fish. Arrange the anchovies, cut into strips, over the salad. Transport in a sealed container. Put the dressing ingredients in a small screw-top jar and transport separately. Shake to blend, pour over the salad before serving.

GREEK SALAD

1 bibb or iceberg lettuce
¼ white cabbage, finely shredded
4 tomatoes, cubed
½ cucumber, cubed
¾ cup black olives
1 cup feta cheese
DRESSING
¾ cup olive oil
1 tablespoon wine vinegar
¼ teaspoon sugar
1 teaspoon fresh basil or oregano, chopped

Combine the lettuce, torn into pieces, cabbage, tomatoes and cucumber in a large container. Sprinkle over the olives and cheese. Chill thoroughly.

Beat the dressing ingredients together and put into a screw-top jar. Dress the salad just before serving.

MOZZARELLA AND TOMATO SALAD

SERVES 6-8

3 cups Mozzarella cheese
4 sweet, ripe tomatoes
8 black peppercorns, crushed
10 small fresh basil leaves
olive oil for dressing

Slice the cheese and the tomatoes and arrange them in a container, overlapping, in circles. Sprinkle over the peppercorns, olives and basil. Cover.

Just before serving season with a little salt and sprinkle with olive oil.

KIWI CITRUS FRUIT SALAD

SERVES 6-8

4 oranges, peeled, segmented, all pith removed
1 grapefruit, peeled, segmented, all pith removed
4 kiwi fruit, peeled and sliced
1 lime, grated rind and juice
3 tablespoons superfine sugar
¾ cup water
1-2 tablespoons kirsch liqueur
few drops rose water

Mix the orange, grapefruit and kiwi fruit. Place the lime rind and juice, sugar and water in a small pan. Heat gently to dissolve the sugar and bring to the boil for 2 minutes. Cool and stir in the kirsch and a few drops of rose water. Pour over the fruit and chill. Transport in a sealed container.

CASSATA

SERVES 6-8

1¼ cups milk
1¼ cups heavy cream
4 egg yolks
½ cup superfine sugar
¾ cup heavy cream, whipped
1 orange, grated rind and juice
few drops orange coloring
2 tablespoons raisins
¼ cup candied peel, chopped
¼ cup candied cherries, chopped
2 tablespoons Madeira wine
½ cup raspberry sherbet

Bring the milk and heavy cream to the boil and remove from the heat. Beat the egg yolks and sugar together in a large shallow bowl until thick and light. Stir in the scalded milk and cream. Set over a pan of simmering water and cook, stirring frequently until the mixture has thickened enough to coat the back of a wooden spoon. Remove from the heat and cover the surface of the custard with plastic wrap, to prevent a skin forming. Cool.

Fold the whipped cream into the custard then reserve one third of the mixture. To the remainder add the orange rind and juice and a few drops of coloring. Add the raisins, peel, cherries and Madeira wine to the reserved portion. Freeze separately until mushy. Beat until smooth and refreeze. Soften the orange ice cream and spread it round the sides of a chilled metal mold or bowl lined with plastic wrap. Freeze until firm. Soften the tutti frutti ice cream and spread over the orange ice cream leaving a central hole. Pack the sherbert into this. Freeze until solid.

To transport, pack in an insulated freezer box or bag with several ice packs or dry ice. Before serving, unmold the ice cream and peel away the plastic wrap. Serve in slices with wafers.

POACHED PEARS

SERVES 6-8

6-8 firm pears
1 lemon
1 orange
6 cloves
4 allspice berries
1¼ cups red wine
2 tablespoons port
3 tablespoons superfine sugar
1 small cinnamon stick

Peel the pears but leave the stalks attached. Remove the cores from the base end using a small teaspoon. Pare the rind thinly from the lemon and orange and place in a pan with the pears. Add the juice from the fruit and the cloves, allspice and wine. Bring the liquid to a very slow simmer and poach for 20 to 30 minutes until the pears are tender. Turn the pears occasionally so that they take up an even red color. Remove the pears, rind and spices with a slotted spoon. Allow the pears to cool.

Add the port, sugar and cinnamon to the pan and stir to dissolve the sugar. Bring to the boil and simmer until the syrup is thickened and reduced. Remove the cinnamon stick and cool the syrup.

Transport the pears in a sealed container with the syrup. Serve with light cream.

DARK AND WHITE CHOCOLATE MOUSSE

SERVES 4-6

Take great care when melting white chocolate – it very quickly turns into hard lumps if even slightly overheated. Shave into a heat-proof pitcher and stand it in a bowl of hot, not boiling, water. Stir until the chocolate has melted.

3 eggs, separated
¼ cup superfine sugar
¾ cup semisweet chocolate, melted
½ cup white chocolate, very gently melted
2 tablespoons Cointreau
¾ cup heavy cream, whipped

Beat the egg yolks in a large bowl with the sugar until very thick and pale. Fold in the semisweet chocolate. In another bowl, beat the egg whites until stiff. Mix together the white chocolate, Cointreau and cream and fold in the egg whites. Spoon the two mixtures alternately into small serving containers with lids and swirl with a knife tip to give a marbled effect. Chill until set. Cover for transporting. Serve with wafers.

OLIVE AND ANCHOVY BREAD

MAKES 2 LOAVES

I cake compressed yeast
2 cups hand-hot water
I Vitamin C tablet (ascorbic acid), crushed
6 cups all-purpose flour
¼ cup black olives, pitted and roughly chopped
¼ cup green olives, pitted and roughly chopped
I tablespoon dried oregano
½ oz anchovies, drained and chopped

Blend the yeast, water and the vitamin C tablet together. Sift the flour into a warmed bowl. Stir in the olives, oregano and anchovies. Add the yeast liquid and mix to a dough. Knead on a floured surface until very soft, smooth and elastic. Shape the dough into two flat round loaves. Place on a greased baking sheet. Cover with oiled plastic wrap and allow to rise in a warm place until doubled in size (about I hour).

Remove the plastic and sprinkle the loaves with a little more flour. Bake at 450°F for 20-30 minutes until they sound hollow when tapped underneath and are golden brown. Cool on a wire rack and serve broken into chunks.

ROSEMARY BREAD STICKS

MAKES 18

½ cake compressed yeast
I cup hand-hot water
½ Vitamin C tablet (ascorbic acid), crushed
3 cups all-purpose flour
I teaspoon salt
2 teaspoons sugar
I tablespoon butter
I teaspoon rosemary
2 tablespoons olive oil
2 tablespoons tomato paste
¾ cup boiling water
I teaspoon ground rosemary

Blend the yeast and the water. Stir in the crushed vitamin C tablet. Sift the flour, salt and sugar into a warmed bowl. Rub in the butter. Stir in the yeast liquid and rosemary. Mix to a soft dough then knead on a lightly-floured surface for about 10 minutes. The dough should be smooth and elastic. Divide the dough into three pieces. Roll each out to a thin round the size of a dinner plate. Place each on a greased baking sheet. Cover with oiled plastic wrap and leave to rise in a warm place for about 50 minutes until doubled in size.

Brush the rounds with olive oil. Blend the tomato paste with the boiling water and stir in the ground rosemary. Spread this mixture over the breads. Slash the breads across deeply into wide fingers. Bake at 425°F for 15 to 20 minutes until risen and golden underneath. Allow to cool on wire racks.

Transport the bread sticks in paper bags and tear into fingers to serve.

VARIATION   *Saffron Bread*
Make the basic dough as for Rosemary Bread Sticks but substitute 2 pinches of powdered saffron for the rosemary. Shape the dough into two round loaves. After proving, brush with milk and sprinkle with cream of wheat. Slash the tops of the dough into diamond shapes and bake for 30 to 40 minutes. Break off large chunks to serve.

JAPONAISE FINGERS

MAKES 12

2 egg whites
½ cup superfine sugar
I cup ground almonds
FILLING
½ cup semisweet chocolate
I teaspoon coffee extract
½ cup heavy cream

Beat the egg whites until very stiff. Gradually sprinkle in two-thirds of the sugar while continuing to beat, until the mixture is very stiff and glossy. Fold in the remaining sugar and almonds using a spatula. Spoon into a large pastry bag fitted with a large plain nozzle and pipe 24 fingers on a greased and lined cookie sheet. Bake at 325°F for 45 minutes without browning. Cool on a wire rack. To make the filling, place all the ingredients in a bowl and set over a pan of simmering water. Cook until melted and stir to blend. Cool. Whip the mixture until thick and fluffy and use to sandwich the fingers together in twos. Chill until set. Pack into a rigid container.

VARIATION   *Japonaise Cakes*
Make as for Japonaise Fingers but pipe the mixture into small flat rounds instead of fingers.

For the filling, cream together ½ cup sweet butter, 1½ cups confectioners' sugar and 2 teaspoons coffee extract. Sandwich the rounds with a little filling and pipe a small rosette of it on top of each cake. Finish each cake with a hazelnut on top.

FLORENTINES

MAKES 18

¼ cup butter
3 tablespoons superfine sugar
I cup blanched almonds, chopped
¼ cup candied peel, chopped
¼ cup candied cherries, chopped
I tablespoon light cream
½ cup semisweet chocolate pieces, melted

Place the butter and sugar in a small pan and heat gently until melted. Add the nuts, peel, cherries and cream. Drop small spoonfuls of the mixture, well spaced, on to cookie sheets lined with parchment paper. Cook at 375°F for 8-9 minutes. Leave to cool on the cookie sheets for 2 to 3 minutes then neaten the edges of the Florentines with a round pastry cutter. Lift from the paper with a palette knife and cool on a wire rack. When cool spread the flat sides of the Florentines with melted chocolate and mark in wavy lines with a fork. Leave to set.

Pack, interleaved with waxed paper, in a rigid container.

CHILDREN'S PICNICS

The novelty of eating outside – on the grass or perched on a rock – is half the fun of a picnic, and children appreciate this perhaps better than anyone. Almost any outside space is suitable, but best are those with plenty of room for games and adventures.

With no rug to spill food on, nothing valuable to break and no party clothes to ruin, adults can relax while children run wild. The food can reflect this mood of excitement. Spiral-shaped Sausage Twirls, Tomato and Egg Butterflies and Eggy Buns fit in with the party spirit. Bite-sized Barbecue Chicken Chunks, Mini Bacon Quiches and Cheesy Cookies are perfect for eating on the run. As the party winds down, a selection of brightly-colored Cupcakes and cream-filled Chocolate Boxes provide a wonderful final surprise.

CHEESY COOKIES

SERVES 8-10

2 cups all-purpose flour
½ cup cream of wheat
1 teaspoon salt
pinch cayenne pepper
1¼ cups Cheddar cheese, very finely grated
1 cup butter
FILLING
1 cup cream cheese
½ cup unflavored yogurt
2 tablespoons smooth peanut butter

Mix the flour, cream of wheat, salt and pepper in a bowl. Stir in the cheese and rub in the butter until the mixture resembles fine bread crumbs. Chill for 30 minutes. Knead the mixture with the hands to a firm dough. Roll out to ¼ inch thick on a surface dusted with cream of wheat. Cut out with small pastry cutters and transfer to a greased baking sheet. Bake at 350°F for 25 minutes. Cool on a wire rack. To make the filling, cream together all the ingredients and use to sandwich two sides together.

Chill before packing into a rigid container.

BARBECUE CHICKEN CHUNKS

SERVES 6-8

2 tablespoons thick honey
1 tablespoon light brown sugar
1 tablespoon white wine vinegar
1 tablespoon tomato paste
¾ cup orange juice
1 tablespoon soy sauce
1 teaspoon Worcestershire sauce
pinch dry mustard
3-4 chicken breasts, skinned, boned and cut into chunks

Place the honey, sugar, vinegar, tomato paste, orange juice, sauces and mustard in a small pan. Bring to the boil and simmer for 10 minutes. The sauce should be of a syrupy consistency. Season with ground black pepper. Remove from the heat and stir the chicken pieces into the sauce. Remove them with tongs and set on a rack in a broiling pan. Broil for 10 minutes, brushing with the sauce and turning frequently.

Allow to cool and pack in a rigid container.

SAUSAGE TWIRLS

SERVES 6-8

2 cups all-purpose flour
½ cup butter
1 teaspoon dry mustard
large pinch salt
1 lb small sausages, cooked and cooled
beaten egg

Sift the flour into a bowl and rub in the butter. Stir in the mustard and salt. Add just enough water to bind to a firm dough (about 3½ tablespoons).

Wrap in plastic wrap and chill for 30 minutes. Roll out thinly on a lightly-floured work surface and cut into long strips about ¼ inch wide. Brush with beaten egg and roll the strips round the sausages to give a spiral effect. Brush the pastry with beaten egg. Place on a greased baking sheet and bake at 400°F for 10 to 15 minutes. Cool on a wire rack.

Pack in a rigid container with mild mustard for dipping for those who want it.

CHEESE BAGELS

MAKES 12

½ cake compressed yeast
1¼ cups hand-hot water
4 cups whole wheat flour
1½ teaspoons salt
2 tablespoons butter
1¼ cups Cheddar cheese, grated
beaten egg
2 tablespoons poppy seeds

Blend the yeast and water together. Mix the flour and salt together in a warmed bowl. Rub in the butter. Stir in the cheese. Pour in the yeast liquid and mix until the mixture leaves the sides of the bowl. Turn out the dough on to a floured work surface. Knead for about 10 minutes until very smooth, soft and elastic. Divide the dough into 12 pieces and shape each into small flat rounds. Make a hole in the center of each to form rings. Poach the rings in a large pan of simmering water for about 20 seconds until they start to puff up. Remove them with a flexible metal spatula and place on greased baking sheets. Cover with oiled plastic wrap and allow to rise in a warm place for 1 hour. Brush with beaten egg and sprinkle with poppy seeds. Bake at 450°F for 10-15 minutes. Cool on a wire rack. Split and butter before packing.

TOMATO AND EGG BUTTERFLIES

MAKES 16

½ lb puff pastry
1 egg yolk
1 tablespoon tomato paste
1 teaspoon yeast extract

Roll out the pastry to a rectangle 12 by 8 inches. Cut into four 8 by 3-inch strips. Beat together the egg yolk, tomato paste and yeast extract. Brush down the center of three of the strips. Place three strips on top of each other, with the egg yolk upwards, matching the edges to form a neat stack. Lay the unbrushed strip on top. Press the stack down the center with a rolling pin to seal them together. Cut the stack across into 16 slices, 3 inches long and ½ inch thick. Place the slices on a greased cookie sheet. Bake at 425°F for 15 minutes. Cool on a wire rack before packing in a rigid container.

EGGY BUNS

SERVES 8-10

¾ cup water
¼ cup butter
½ cup, plus 2 teaspoons all-purpose flour
pinch dry mustard
2 eggs, beaten
2 tablespoons Parmesan cheese, grated
FILLING
3 hard-cooked eggs, shelled, mashed
2 tablespoons butter, melted
2 tablespoons mayonnaise
1 tablespoon fresh parsley, chopped

Place the water and butter in a small pan and heat until the butter melts. Bring to the boil and add the flour. Beat for 1 minute over the heat, to a smooth mixture. Stir in the mustard. Allow to cool slightly. Gradually beat in the eggs, to make a smooth, glossy paste that just holds its shape. Spoon into a pastry bag fitted with a large plain nozzle. Pipe small rounds on to greased baking sheets and sprinkle each with a little Parmesan cheese.

Bake at 425°F for 20 to 25 minutes until crisp and browned. Cool on a wire rack.

To make the filling, mix the ingredients together and check the seasoning. Chill.

Just before packing, split the buns and fill each with a little of the mixture.

MINI BACON QUICHES

MAKES 12

1 cup all-purpose flour
1 cup self-rising whole wheat flour
½ cup butter
pinch of salt
about 1 cup iced water
FILLING
1 tablespoon oil
6 slices bacon, derinded and chopped
1 onion, peeled and chopped
1¼ cups Cheddar cheese, diced
¾ cup heavy cream
6 tablespoons milk
2 eggs
¼ cup canned corn, drained

Place the flours in a bowl and rub in the butter. Stir in the salt and enough water to bind to a firm dough. Knead lightly and roll out on a floured surface. Cut out rounds with a pastry cutter and use to line the cups in a muffin pan.

To make the filling, heat the oil in a pan and fry the bacon and onion together for 4 minutes. Drain and place in the bowl of a food processor with the cheese, cream, milk and eggs. Add salt and freshly-ground white pepper. Work for a few seconds to finely chop and mix the ingredients. Stir in the corn and divide the mixture between the pastry cups. Bake at 375°F for 20 to 25 minutes until set and golden brown. Cool on a wire rack.

Pack in a rigid container layered with paper towelling.

SAVORY PUFF FINGERS

SERVES 8-10

¾ lb puff pastry
1 tablespoon yeast extract
1 tablespoon boiling water
2 tablespoons sesame seeds

Roll out the pastry thinly on a floured surface to a large rectangle. Blend the yeast extract with the water and brush all over the surface of the pastry. Sprinkle with the seeds and press them on. Cut into strips about 5 by ½ inch. Twist each strip several times from both ends and lay on baking sheets. Bake at 375°F for 10 minutes until golden brown and crisp. Cool on a wire rack and pack into rigid containers for transporting.

EGG AND WATER CRESS MINI LOAVES

MAKES 8

8 miniature whole wheat loaves
4 hard-cooked eggs
¼ cup mayonnaise
½ bunch water cress, chopped
pinch paprika
1 teaspoon lemon juice

Cut a slice from the top of the mini loaves and reserve. Scoop out the crumb from inside the loaves with a pointed teaspoon. Season inside the loaves with salt and pepper. Chop the eggs roughly and mix with mayonnaise, water cress, pepper and lemon juice. Pile into the loaves and replace the tops. Pack in a rigid container and chill before transporting.

CHEESE FRUIT AND NUT NIBBLES

SERVES 6-8

4 red-colored apples, cored, cut into dice
2 green-colored apples, cored, cut into dice
2 tablespoons lemon juice
⅓ cup white raisins
½ cup shelled peanuts
2½ cups Cheddar cheese, cut into dice

Place the apples and lemon juice in a container and mix so that the apples are coated in juice. Add the white raisins, nuts and cheese. Chill. Seal the container for transporting.

HERBY SAUSAGES AND MUSTARD DIP

SERVES 6-8

½ lb herby cocktail sausages
DIP
6 tablespoons mayonnaise
6 tablespoons thick unflavored yogurt
1-2 tablespoons mild prepared mustard
2 tablespoons ketchup
1 tablespoon onion, finely chopped
1 tablespoon fresh parsley, chopped

Place the sausages in a roasting pan and bake at 400°F for about 20 minutes. Drain them thoroughly on paper toweling. Cool and pack into a rigid container with toothpicks for spearing.

For the dip, blend all the ingredients and pack into a small sealed container.

CHEESE AND CELERY NUT BREAD

MAKES 1 LOAF

2 cups self-rising flour, sifted
pinch dry mustard
¼ cup butter
1¼ cups Cheddar cheese, grated
¾ cup celery, finely chopped
½ cup walnuts, coarsley chopped
1 tablespoon oil
½ onion peeled and chopped
3 slices bacon, without rinds and chopped
2 tablespoons fresh parsley, chopped
1 egg, beaten
¾ cup milk

Place the flour and mustard in a bowl. Rub in the butter and stir in the cheese, celery and nuts. Heat the oil in a pan and fry the onion and bacon for 3 minutes. Drain and cool. Add to the flour. Beat the parsley, egg and milk together. Stir into the flour mixture and mix to a soft dough. Turn into a greased and lined 2 lb loaf pan and smooth the top. Bake at 375°F for 1 hour until risen and golden. Cool in the pan for 20 minutes. Turn out on to a wire rack.

Slice and butter before packing.

STRAWBERRY CUPCAKES

MAKES 12

½ cup butter
½ cup superfine sugar
2 eggs, beaten
1 cup self-rising flour
few drops pink food coloring
TOPPING
½ cup white chocolate, very gently melted
(see page 41)
2 tablespoons butter
½ cup confectioners' sugar
few drops red coloring
boiling water

Cream together the butter and sugar until light and fluffy. Gradually beat in the eggs and finally fold in the flour and enough food coloring to make the mixture dark pink. (The coloring fades when baked so add a little more than you think necessary.) Divide between 12 paper baking cups set in cupcake pans. Knock the pan on the work surface to distribute the mixture evenly. Bake at 350°F for 10 to 15 minutes until golden brown. Remove from the oven and cool on a wire rack. To make the topping, blend the chocolate and butter and smooth over the cakes to make a flat surface inside the paper baking cups. Blend the confectioners' sugar with a few drops of coloring and boiling water to make a thick consistency. Pipe thin parallel lines of the frosting over the chocolate. Draw the end of a skewer backwards and forwards through the frosting to create a feathered pattern. Allow to set in a cool place. Pack the cakes in a rigid container in one layer.

VARIATION   *Lemon Cupcakes*
Make as for the Strawberry Cupcakes but use the finely-grated rind of 1 lemon instead of coloring in the cake. For the frosting, use lemon juice in place of water and color it with a few drops of yellow food coloring.

CHOCOLATE BOXES

MAKES 9

2 cups semisweet or milk chocolate, melted
6 in square slab plain sponge cake
apricot jelly, warmed and sieved
¾ cup heavy cream, whipped
decorative miniature marzipan fruits

Spread the chocolate out thinly over a large sheet of parchment paper or waxed paper. Leave to set in a cool dry place. Cut the sponge cake into 9 smaller squares. Cut the set chocolate into squares to fit the sides and tops of the cake squares. Spread the sides of the sponge cakes with jelly. Remove the chocolate squares from the paper and press them on to the sides and bottom of the cake squares. Pipe or pile whipped cream on top of the cake squares, add a marzipan fruit and set a final chocolate square at an angle on the cream as the lid. Chill well. Pack closely in one layer in a rigid container and keep cool.

CARAMEL FINGERS

MAKES 14

1 cup butter
1½ cups all-purpose flour
¾ cup superfine sugar
1 7 oz can sweetened condensed milk
2 tablespoons light corn syrup
1 cup semisweet chocolate, melted

Rub half the butter into the flour, until the mixture resembles bread crumbs. Stir in ¼ cup of the sugar. Knead the mixture with the hands until it comes together to form a smooth dough. Press it evenly into a greased 7 by 11-inch jelly roll pan. Bake at 350°F for 20 minutes until golden. Cool in the pan. In a saucepan place the remaining butter, sugar, milk and syrup. Heat gently then bring to the boil for about 5 minutes, stirring continuously. The sugar will caramelize and the mixture should turn a pale brown. Remove from the heat and beat for 2 to 3 minutes. Pour on to the cooled cake in the pan and leave to cool and set. Spread the melted chocolate over the surface and mark with a fork. Mark into fingers and allow to set. Cut into bars.

Transport in the pan layered in paper toweling and keep as cool as possible.

LIME AND STRAWBERRY JELLY MOUSSE

SERVES 8-10

1 packet lime jelly
1 packet strawberry jelly
14 oz can evaporated milk, chilled overnight
DECORATION
sugar dots

Make up the jellies as directed on the pack but add only enough water to make 1 pint. Allow the jellies to cool. In a clean, cool bowl, beat the evaporated milk until it becomes very thick and frothy. Divide it into two portions. Just as the jellies are beginning to thicken, beat each into a portion of evaporated milk. Quickly spoon the mixtures alternately into clear plastic drinking containers. Swirl the desserts with the end of a wooden spoon to marble the colors together. Chill until completely set.

Sprinkle the top with sugar dots just before serving.

LEMON MERINGUE ICE CREAM

SERVES 6-8

¾ cup water
½ cup, plus 2 teaspoons superfine sugar
3 eggs, separated
¾ cup heavy cream, whipped
2 meringue shells, roughly crushed
2 graham crackers, roughly crushed
1 lemon, grated rind and juice
6-8 crisp wafer cones

Place the water and sugar in a small pan and heat gently, stirring until the sugar has dissolved. Bring to the boil, without stirring and boil to 225°F. Beat the egg yolks until pale and thick and then gradually beat in the hot syrup, pouring it in a thin stream. Continue to beat until the mixture has cooled and thickened. Fold in the whipped cream, meringue, graham crackers and lemon rind and juice. Finally beat the egg whites until stiff and fold in. Pour into a shallow freezer container and freeze until solid. Spoon the ice cream into crisp wafer cones and re-freeze.

Transport the cones in insulated freezer bags or boxes, packed with ice packs.

FRESH LEMON AND LIME PUNCH

SERVES 6-8

3 lemons
3 limes
1½ cups sugar
scant 1 cup water

Scrub the fruit in hot water. Grate the rinds finely and squeeze the juice. Place the rind and sugar in a pan. Add the water and heat gently, stirring, until the sugar has dissolved. Bring to the boil and cook for 2 minutes. Allow to cool and stir in the fruit juice. Strain and chill. Transport in a sealed bottle and dilute with iced or mineral water to serve.

FOOD FOR LOVE

A well-planned picnic can be one of the most romantic ways of celebrating for two. Tempting delicacies can be prepared in advance, leaving plenty of time to talk and relax.

Choose light, attractive dishes which reflect the romance of the occasion. The combination of shrimp, mace, root ginger, lemon juice, Tabasco sauce and chives makes Spicy Potted Shrimp a memorable starter. Follow, perhaps, with Chicken Tikka Pieces which come skewered like a kebab and garnished with lemon wedges to make a spectacular display. Cut the Crab and Chicken Roll into spiral-shaped slices and serve with a light salad as an alternative.

The Orange and Rosewater Bavarois, decorated with sugared rose petals, makes an appropriately dreamy dessert. Then, for a final touch of elegance, present a pretty dish full of Frosting-dipped Fruits.

SALMON AND CREAM CHEESE MOUSSE

SERVES 2

½ lb can of salmon, drained
1¼ cups liquid aspic
½ cup cream cheese, softened
I hard-cooked egg, chopped
I lemon, grated rind and juice
2 tablespoons mayonnaise
2 tablespoons fresh parsley, chopped
few drops Tabasco sauce
salt, pepper
GARNISH
fresh shrimp

Place the salmon and aspic in a food processor or blender and work until smooth. Stir in the cream cheese and the remaining ingredients. Season and pour into an oiled fish-shaped mold. Chill until set. Transport in the mold and turn out just before serving. Garnish with shrimp.

SPICY POTTED SHRIMP

APPETIZER   SERVES 2

¾ cup small shrimp, shelled
pinch ground mace
½ teaspoon green ginger, freshly grated
few drops lemon juice
few drops Tabasco sauce
I tablespoon fresh chives, chopped
¾ cup butter, melted

Mix together the shrimp, mace, ginger, lemon juice, Tabasco and chives. Put ¼ cup of the butter in a pan and add the shrimp mixture. Stir over a very gentle heat until the butter is absorbed. Season with freshly-ground white pepper. Spoon the mixture into two custard cups and smooth down. Strain the remaining butter through scalded cheesecloth and pour over the surface of each cup to seal. Chill overnight.

Transport in the cups and serve with thinly-sliced whole wheat bread.

MANGO SOUFFLÉS

SERVES 2

2 eggs separated
3 tablespoons superfine sugar
1 mango, peeled, pit removed, puréed
½ oz unflavored gelatin, dissolved in 3 tablespoons
boiling water, cooled
½ lemon, finely grated rind and juice
¾ cup heavy cream, whipped
DECORATION
slices of lemon

Beat the egg yolks and sugar together until pale and thick. Stir in the mango purée, cooled gelatin, lemon juice and rind. Fold in the whipped cream. Beat the egg whites until stiff and fold in. Pour into individual dishes for transportation and chill until set. Decorate with lemon slices.

CHEESE, CHIVES AND NUT TURNOVERS

MAKES 6

⅔ cup cream cheese, softened
2 tablespoons fresh chives, snipped
½ cup pistachio nuts, chopped
½ teaspoon paprika pepper
6 sheets filo pastry
3 tablespoons olive oil

Blend the cream cheese with the chives, nuts and pepper. Brush a sheet of filo pastry all over with olive oil. Place a spoonful of filling at one end of the pastry and fold and roll the pastry round the filling to make a neat, sausage shape. Place on a baking sheet. Repeat with the remaining pastry and filling. Brush the turnovers again with oil and bake at 400°F for 10 to 15 minutes until golden brown and crisp. Cool on a wire rack. Transport in a rigid container.

CHICKEN TIKKA PIECES

MAIN DISH   SERVES 2

2 chicken breasts, skinned, boned and cut into
chunks
¾ cup unflavored yogurt
pinch chili powder
¼ teaspoon ground ginger
¼ teaspoon tumeric
½ teaspoon freshly-ground coriander seeds
½ teaspoon garlic paste
salt, freshly-ground black pepper
1 tablespoon lemon juice
GARNISH
lemon wedges

Place the chicken pieces in a bowl or plastic bag. Mix together the yogurt, spices, garlic and lemon juice. Season with salt and freshly-ground black pepper. Pour over the chicken and mix well. Cover and marinate overnight in the refrigerator. On the following day thread the chicken pieces on to two skewers and brush with the marinade. Broil for 7 minutes on each side. Cool and pack the skewers in a rigid container with lemon wedges for garnish.

CRAB AND CHICKEN ROLL

MAIN DISH   SERVES 2

3 tablespoons butter
¼ cup all-purpose flour
¾ cup milk
3 eggs, separated
FILLING
½ lb cooked chicken
½ lb crab meat
6 tablespoons mayonnaise
1 teaspoon paprika
¼ teaspoon cayenne pepper
1 lemon, finely-grated rind and juice

Melt the butter in a small pan and stir in the flour. Cook for 1 minute. Gradually blend in the milk until a smooth sauce is formed. Remove from the heat and beat in the egg yolks. Beat the egg whites until stiff and gently fold into the sauce mixture. Spread evenly into a greased and lined 9 by 13-inch jelly roll pan. Bake at 375°F for 15 to 20 minutes until risen and golden brown. Turn out on to parchment paper and trim the crispy edges. Roll up with the paper inside. Allow to cool.

To make the filling, blend all the ingredients together and season with freshly-ground black pepper. Unroll the cooked mixture and remove the paper. Spread the roll with the filling and roll up once more. Cover and chill.

Slice and pack in a rigid container with the slices interleaved with waxed paper.

CUCUMBER, MUSHROOM AND STRAWBERRY SALAD

SERVES 2-4

¼ cucumber, peeled
2 oz small white mushrooms, sliced
DRESSING
¼ lb strawberries, hulled and puréed
2 tablespoons oil
1 teaspoon lemon juice
6 fresh mint leaves, shredded

Slice the cucumber in half lengthways and remove the seeds with the point of a teaspoon. Slice thickly and mix with the mushrooms. Chill. Transport in a small container. To make the dresssing, mix all the ingredients together and transport separately. Pour over the salad just before serving.

BULGAR WHEAT SALAD

SERVES 2-4

1 cup bulgar wheat
2 scallions, trimmed and sliced
3 oz shelled shrimp
1 lemon, grated rind only
3 tablespoons fresh parsley, chopped
pinch of cumin powder
2 tablespoons French dressing

Place the bulgar wheat in a large bowl and cover with lukewarm water for 10 minutes. Squeeze the water out of the wheat and dry with paper toweling. Mix in the remaining ingredients and season with plenty of freshly-ground black pepper. Chill before serving.

GINGERED PEARS WITH CARAMEL

SERVES 2

2 firm pears with stalk left intact
3 tablespoons light brown sugar
¾ cup white wine
1 orange, grated rind and juice
2 pieces preserved stem ginger, sliced
3 tablespoons of the stem ginger syrup
1 cinnamon stick

Remove the base and cores from the pears with a small teaspoon. Place the remaining ingredients in a pan and heat gently, stirring, until the sugar dissolves. Add the pears and poach gently for 15 to 20 minutes until tender. Remove the pears to a container. Bring the contents of the pan to the boil for 5 to 10 minutes until syrupy. Remove the cinnamon stick and pour the syrup over the pears. Chill and serve with half and half cream.

ORANGE AND ROSEWATER BAVAROIS

SERVES 2

2 egg yolks
½ cup confectioners' sugar
¾ cup milk, scalded
few drops rosewater
¼ oz unflavored gelatin
1 tablespoon boiling water
1 orange, finely grated rind and juice
¾ cup heavy cream, whipped
DECORATION
rose petals
egg white
superfine sugar

Beat the egg yolks and sugar in a large bowl until thick and pale. Gradually beat in the milk. Set the bowl over a pan of simmering water and cook, stirring, until the custard is thick enough to coat the back of a wooden spoon. Remove from the heat. Stir in the rosewater. Dissolve the gelatin in the boiling water and add to the custard with the orange rind and juice. Cover the surface with plastic wrap and allow to cool.

Fold the whipped cream into the custard and pour into two small, oiled molds or serving dishes. Chill until set. Transport the bavarois in the molds.

For the decoration, paint both sides of the rose petals with egg white using a small paint brush. Dredge thickly with superfine sugar and shake off the excess. Leave to dry on a paper towel. Pack carefully in a rigid container padded with paper towelling.

Just before serving, ease the set bavarois away from the mold sides with the fingertips and turn out. Decorate with the sugared rose petals.

SPONGE DROPS

MAKES 10

2 eggs
3 tablespoons superfine sugar
½ cup all-purpose flour
few drops vanilla extract
superfine sugar for dredging

Place the eggs and sugar in a large bowl and beat them until they become very thick and foamy. Sift the flour twice and fold into the mixture with a few drops of vanilla extract. Spoon the mixture into a pastry bag fitted with a large plain nozzle and quickly pipe small rounds on to baking sheets lined with waxed paper. Dredge the rounds heavily with superfine sugar and very quickly tilt the paper sideways to remove the excess sugar. Bake the drops at 400°F for 10 to 12 minutes to a pale golden color. Cool on a wire rack. Pack in a rigid container lined with paper toweling.

VARIATION *Sponge Fingers*
Make as for the Sponge Drops but pipe the mixture into fingers instead of rounds. After baking, dip the ends in melted chocolate and allow to set on a wire rack. Pack in a rigid container lined with paper toweling.

FROSTING-DIPPED FRUITS

SERVES 2-4

FROSTING
4 oz granulated sugar
2 tablespoons water
¼ teaspoon liquid glucose
6 oz fresh fruits such as cherries, strawberries
and grapes, with hulls, stalks etc. if possible

To make the frosting, dissolve the sugar in water over gentle heat. Bring to the boil and add the glucose. Boil to 250°F on a sugar thermometer (soft ball stage). Remove from the heat to cool a little, then pour the syrup on to a wetted work surface. Leave for 1 to 2 minutes then, using a wooden spatula, work the syrup from the outside edges to the center until the frosting forms. Knead small pieces with your fingers until smooth. Form a ball and leave to mellow for 1 hour.

Next, place the frosting in a bowl over simmering water. Stir, then add sufficient water to thin the frosting to the consistency of thick cream.

Dip the fruit into the frosting to coat the bottom half. Place on waxed paper to dry. Pack the fruit carefully, at the last moment, layered with waxed paper into a rigid container.

STRAWBERRY AND GOOSEBERRY FOOLS

¼ lb gooseberries
2 tablespoons superfine sugar
2 egg yolks
2 tablespoons confectioners' sugar
1¼ cups creamy milk
¾ cup whipping cream
6 oz strawberries, hulled and puréed
DECORATION
freshly-sliced strawberries

Place the gooseberries, sugar and 1 tablespoon of water in a small, tightly-lidded pan. Set over gentle heat and cook for 5 to 8 minutes until the gooseberries are very tender. Press through a sieve and cool. Place the egg yolks and confectioners' sugar in a large bowl and beat until very thick. Set the bowl over a pan of simmering water and beat in the milk. Cook gently until the custard is thick enough to coat the back of a wooden spoon. Press a sheet of clear plastic wrap over the surface of the custard and leave to cool.

When cold, stir in the gooseberry purée and the cream. Pour into small dishes, swirling the strawberry purée as you go. Chill before serving decorated with strawberries.

CREAMY DUTCH SYLLABUB

¾ cup light cream
¾ cup heavy cream
¾ cup thick unflavored yogurt
2 tablespoons chopped stem ginger
2 tablespoons stem ginger syrup
2 tablespoons advocaat liqueur
1 orange, finely-grated rind only

Mix the light and heavy cream and beat until stiff. Fold in the yogurt. Blend the stem ginger, syrup, liqueur and orange rind. Stir into the cream. Spoon into containers and chill well before the journey. Serve with sponge drops.

MARZIPAN PIES

SERVES 2

¼ lb shortcrust pastry
2 tablespoons raspberry conserve
FILLING
½ oz finely-ground almonds
½ oz marzipan, grated
¼ cup sweet butter
3 tablespoons superfine sugar
I egg, beaten
I oz all-purpose flour
DECORATION
3 tablespoons confectioners' sugar, sifted
1-2 teaspoons lemon juice

Line two 4-inch pie pans with the pastry. Spread the conserve evenly on the base of the pastry.

To make the filling, mix the ground almonds and the marzipan together. Beat the butter with the sugar until light and fluffy. Gradually beat in the egg and finally fold in the flour and almond mixture. Divide between the pastry cases and smooth the mixture on top. Bake at 370°F for 20 to 25 minutes until risen and firm.

As the pies cool in their pans, blend the confectioners' sugar and just enough lemon juice to make a thin cream. Spread over the pies and leave to cool. Transport in the pans.

HERBED FRENCH STICK WITH GARLIC BUTTER

MAKES I LOAF

½ cake compressed yeast
I cup hand-hot milk
½ (25 mg) tablet Vitamin C (ascorbic acid), crushed
3 cups all-purpose flour
I teaspoon salt
2 teaspoons sugar
2 tablespoons butter
I tablespoon fresh chopped parsley
I tablespoon fresh chopped rosemary
I teaspoon fresh chopped thyme
beaten egg
2 tablespoons sesame seeds

Blend the yeast and milk and stir in the crushed vitamin C tablet. Mix the flour, salt and sugar in a warmed bowl. Rub in the butter and stir in the herbs. Pour in the yeast liquid and mix to a soft dough. Knead on a lightly-floured surface for 10 minutes until soft, smooth and elastic. Shape the dough into a long french loaf and place on a greased baking sheet. Cover with oiled plastic wrap and leave to rise in a warm place for about I hour until doubled in size. Remove the wrap, brush with beaten egg and sprinkle with seeds. Bake at 450°F for 15 to 20 minutes until golden brown and sounds hollow when tapped underneath. Cool on a wire rack.

Just before serving, break the loaf into pieces and serve with garlic butter.

GARLIC BUTTER Cream ½ cup butter with I tablespoon garlic paste and I tablespoon freshly-chopped parsley. Form into a neat pat and wrap in foil. Chill.

EXTRAVAGANT ENTERTAINING

Some picnic occasions call for a more formal approach than others. A day at the races, or an elegant garden party are good excuses for a luxuriously sophisticated spread.

Choose dishes to convey the glamor of the event. Pork Satay makes an exotic starter or, alternatively, Mushroom-stuffed Brioches and Savory Stilton Mille Feuilles are tempting with their freshly-baked pastry and delicious fillings.

For the main course, Chicken Galantine, served with a selection of salads, looks and tastes impressive. Choose from Celery, Ham and Carrot Salad, Cold Parslied Ratatouille Salad and Water Cress and Palm Heart Salad for a tasteful combination.

For a final touch, present a spectacular dessert. Both the Special Summer Pudding and the Cœur à la Crème (a heart-shaped dessert served with fresh strawberries or raspberries) would make appropriately flamboyant conclusions.

PORK SATAY

SERVES 4

½ lb pork fillet
2 tablespoons butter
1 tablespoon oil
½ onion, peeled and chopped
2 tablespoons creamed coconut
½ cup boiling water
pinch chili powder
¼ teaspoon turmeric
¼ teaspoon *garam marsala*
2 tablespoons crunchy peanut butter
1 tablespoon lime juice
GARNISH
¼ red bell pepper, shredded
1 tablespoon shredded coconut

Fry the pork fillet in the butter over a moderate heat for about 20 minutes, turning frequently. Drain and cool. Put aside.

Heat the oil and fry the onion until soft. Dissolve the creamed coconut in the boiling water and pour into the onion. Stir in the spices, peanut butter and lime juice. Season with freshly-ground black pepper. Cool. Pack into a sealed container.

Slice the pork into small pieces in a rigid container garnished with the bell pepper and coconut. Supply toothpicks for spearing the pork to dip in the sauce.

MUSHROOM STUFFED BRIOCHES

APPETIZER   MAKES 12

½ cake compressed yeast
¼ cup warm water
1 teaspoon sugar
2¼ cups all-purpose flour, sifted
pinch salt
¼ cup butter
2 eggs, beaten
FILLING
4½ cups flat mushrooms, chopped
6 tablespoons butter
few drops Tabasco sauce
½ cup white wine
1 cup cream cheese
freshly-ground black pepper
beaten egg, to glaze

Blend the yeast with the water. Blend in the sugar and 2 tablespoons of the flour. Cover and leave in a warm place for about 20 minutes until frothy. Mix the remaining flour and salt in a warmed bowl. Rub in the butter. Beat the eggs into the yeast batter and pour into the flour. Blend together and work to a soft dough. Knead on a lightly-floured work surface until soft, smooth and elastic. Place in an oiled plastic bag and leave to rise in a warm place until doubled in size. This should take about 1 to 1½ hours.

To make the filling, cook the mushrooms in the butter, Tabasco sauce and wine for 6 minutes. Boil rapidly until the juices are reduced to 2 table-spoons. Stir in the cream cheese and season with freshly-ground black pepper. Cool. Knock back the risen brioche dough and divide into 12 equal pieces. Grease 12 brioche pans.

Cut a quarter off one piece of dough. Flatten the remaining dough into a circle. Place a tablespoon of filling in the center and bring the dough up to completely enclose the filling. Form into a ball. Place in a prepared pan. Form the small piece of dough into a ball shape and press into the center of the brioche in the pan. Repeat with the remaining 11 pieces of dough and filling. Place the brioches on a baking sheet and cover with oiled plastic wrap. Leave in a warm place to prove (about 30 minutes) until puffy. Brush each with beaten egg and bake at 425°F for 15 to 20 minutes until golden brown. Remove from the pans and cool on a wire rack. Pack the brioches in a rigid container and serve with fresh green salad.

SAVORY STILTON MILLE FEUILLES

APPETIZER   SERVES 6-8

¾ lb puff pastry
FILLING
2 cups low-fat cream cheese
¼ cup mayonnaise
1¼ cups Stilton cheese, rind removed
2 tablespoons fresh chives, chopped
GARNISH
walnuts, chopped

Roll the pastry out on a floured surface to ¼ inch thick and cut into three large rectangles. Place on wetted baking sheets and chill for 15 minutes. Prick all over with a fork and bake at 425°F for 15 to 20 minutes until risen and golden. Trim the edges neatly and cool on a wire rack.

To make the filling, soften the low-fat cream cheese in a bowl with the mayonnaise. Crumble in the Stilton and stir into the mixture with the chives. Season with freshly-ground black pepper. Spread each of the pastry rectangles with one third of the mixture. Layer up the pastry pieces into a neat stack. Sprinkle the top with chopped walnuts and chill.

Cut into slices before packing between sheets of waxed paper in a rigid container.

CRAB AND ALMOND QUICHE

SERVES 4-6

PASTRY
2 oz sweet butter
1 cup all-purpose flour
1 teaspoon paprika pepper
1 teaspoon whole grain mustard powder
2-3 tablespoons iced water
FILLING
3 eggs, beaten
1 cup half and half cream
2 scallions, trimmed and sliced
7 oz white crabmeat, drained
1 tablespoon tomato paste
1 teaspoon paprika pepper
few drops Tabasco sauce
pinch of chili powder
¼ cup flaked almonds, toasted

To make the pastry, rub the butter into the flour. Stir in the pepper and mustard and just enough water to make a firm dough. Wrap in clear plastic wrap and chill for 20 minutes. Roll out the pastry thinly and use to line an 8-inch pie pan.

To make the filling, beat together the eggs and cream. Stir in the scallions, crabmeat and remaining ingredients. Pour gently into the pastry case and bake at 350°F for 25-30 minutes. Cool and transport in the pan. Cut into slices to serve.

CHICKEN AND SPINACH ROLLS

SERVES 6

6 chicken breasts, skinned and boned
4 oz frozen chopped spinach, defrosted and
drained to remove excess liquid
1 tablespoon egg white
1 teaspoon ground nutmeg
pinch of cumin powder
2 tablespoons pistachio nuts, finely
chopped
½ cup white wine
freshly-ground black pepper
SAUCE
1¼ cups thick Greek yogurt
1 lemon, grated rind and juice
GARNISH
lambs lettuce

Carefully remove the loose fillet from the underside of each chicken breast and reserve. Place the breasts between sheets of plastic wrap and beat with a rolling pin until flattened to about ¼-inch thick. Remove the wrap. Place the reserved fillets in a food processor with the spinach, egg white, nutmeg, cumin and nuts. Blend until smooth. Divide the filling between the breasts and spread evenly over each. Roll up the chicken to make neat shapes and place on a piece of foil. Sprinkle with wine and plenty of freshly-ground black pepper. Seal the foil packages.

Bake at 350°F for 25 minutes. Allow to cool in the foil. Remove to a rigid container for transportation. Mix the sauce ingredients and transport separately.

SERVING SUGGESTION Serve the chicken in slices garnished with lambs lettuce.

GARLIC AND HAZELNUT ROAST TURKEY

SERVES 8-10

12 lb oven-ready turkey
salt, pepper
1 onion, finely chopped
1-2 cloves garlic, crushed
1 lemon, finely-grated rind and juice
2 tablespoons fresh oregano, chopped
6 oz cream cheese, softened
4 oz fresh bread crumbs
2 oz hazelnuts, chopped
2 oz butter, melted

Rinse and pat dry the turkey. Season the cavity. Mix the onion, garlic, lemon rind and juice, oregano, cheese, bread crumbs and nuts. Place the turkey with the neck towards you. Insert your fingers between the flesh and breast skin. Carefully loosen the skin from the breast and thighs. Spread the stuffing evenly under the skin, reshape and truss the bird. Weigh the bird. Allow 20 minutes per 1 lb cooking time plus 20 minutes. Place in a roasting pan with a rack and brush all over with the melted butter. Roast at 375°F until golden and tender. Allow to cool completely. Wrap in foil and carve at the picnic site for a really glamorous centerpiece.

CHICKEN GALANTINE

MAIN DISH   SERVES UP TO 12

1 4½ lb chicken or capon
1 cup sliced tongue
1½ lb sausage meat
¼ lb bacon, without rind, chopped
1 cup fresh white bread crumbs
1 lemon, grated rind and juice
2 teaspoons dried mixed herbs
1 egg
¾ cup sliced cooked ham
½ cup stuffed green olives, chopped
¼ cup butter, melted
1 tablespoon oil

Bone the bird without breaking the skin. Trim the legs to the lowest joint. Set the bird on a board, breast side down. Make a cut from the tail end, along the backbone to the neck vent. This is the only time you will cut the skin. Using a sharp knife carefully cut the flesh away from the bones of the carcass working either side of the first cut until you reach the leg joints. Cut through these and continue cutting the flesh away from the carcass, cutting through the wing joints until you are able to lift away the main carcass of the bird. Scrape down around the top leg and wing bones to the joints, cut through and remove the bones.

Spread the bird out flat on the board and cover with plastic wrap. Beat several times with a rolling pin to even out the flesh. Season the flesh and cover it with a layer of sliced tongue.

In a large bowl place the sausage meat, bacon, bread crumbs, rind and juice, herbs and egg. Knead together with the hands until evenly blended. Form into a flattened log shape and lay down the center of the bird from neck to tail. Cover the stuffing with slices of ham and finally lay a line of chopped olives down the center of the ham. Season well. Bring the sides of the bird up over the stuffing to enclose it and sew up the skin using a large needle and coarse thread. Turn the bird over and reshape it with the hands. Truss the bird round the legs and wings. Season and set it on a large piece of foil. Brush all over with the butter and oil.

Enclose it in the foil and weigh the package to calculate cooking time.

Place the parcel in a roasting pan and cook at 350°F for 30 minutes per 1 lb. Open the foil and baste well and continue to cook for a further 40 minutes until the skin is golden. To test if the bird is cooked, insert 2 skewers; juices should run clear when cooked. Remove from the foil and leave on a roasting rack to drain and cool. Remove the thread from the skin. Chill.

CELERY, HAM AND CARROT SALAD

SERVES 4-6

8 sticks celery, trimmed and sliced
6 carrots, coarsely grated
8 slices cooked ham, cut into strips
3 tablespoons capers, drained
DRESSING
1¼ cups light cream
1 lemon, finely-grated rind and 1 tablespoon of juice
½ cup unflavored yogurt
pinch ground cumin
freshly-ground black pepper

Place the celery, carrots, ham and capers in a container. Blend the dressing ingredients together and season with freshly-ground black pepper. Mix into the salad and chill well before packing.

COLD PARSLIED RATATOUILLE SALAD

SERVES 6-8

1 eggplant, thickly sliced
salt
3 tablespoons olive oil
2 onions, peeled, sliced
1 lb zucchini, sliced
1 red bell pepper, cored, deseeded and sliced
1 green bell pepper, cored, deseeded and sliced
2 14 oz cans tomatoes
2 teaspoons dried oregano
freshly-ground black pepper
GARNISH
croûtons
¼ cup fresh parsley, chopped
1 tablespoon fresh basil, chopped
black olives

Layer the eggplant slices in a colander with salt. Allow to stand and drain for 30 minutes.

Heat the oil in a large pan. Fry the onion for 3 minutes. Stir in the zucchini and pepper slices and continue to fry for 5 minutes. Rinse the eggplant and add to the pan with the tomatoes and herbs. Season generously with freshly-ground black pepper. Cover the pan and cook gently for 45 minutes. Remove from the heat, cover and cool. Pack into a large container. Chill thoroughly. Serve scattered with croûtons, parsley, basil and olives which have been separately packed.

CRUNCHY CAULIFLOWER SALAD

SERVES 2-4

I large head broccoli
I small cauliflower
I red bell pepper, cored, deseeded and cut into strips
3 oz smoked ham, cut into shreds
½ cup pine nuts, toasted
DRESSING
2 tablespoons raspberry vinegar
½ cup olive oil
pinch of salt
pinch of sugar
I teaspoon whole grain mustard
I tablespoon fresh parsley, chopped

Cut the broccoli and cauliflower into tiny florets. Steam with red bell pepper for 2 to 3 minutes until very lightly cooked and tender but still crunchy. Cool. Mix with the ham and pine nuts. Mix the dressing ingredients together and pour over the salad. Chill before serving.

TORTELLINI AND SOUR CREAM SALAD

½ lb fresh spinach and ham-stuffed tortellini
½ cup sour cream
½ cup thick unflavored yogurt
2 tablespoons mayonnaise
2 tablespoons fresh mint, chopped
½ teaspoon coriander, freshly-ground

Cook the fresh tortellini in boiling salted water for 4 to 6 minutes until tender. Drain and refresh in cold water. Drain.

Blend the sour cream, yogurt, mayonnaise, mint and coriander. Season with ground black pepper and salt. Stir in the pasta and chill. Pack the salad in a rigid container.

WATER CRESS AND PALM HEART SALAD

SERVES 4-6

4 small canned palm hearts, drained and sliced
½ bunch water cress, trimmed
2 thin slices smoked ham, cut into strips
2 tomatoes, sliced
DRESSING
2 tablespoons olive oil
I tablespoon whole grain mustard
few drops lemon juice
pinch sugar

Gently combine the salad ingredients and pack in a rigid container. Chill. Place the dressing ingredients in a small screw-top jar and pack separately. Shake the jar to blend the dressing and pour over the salad just before serving.

BLUE CHEESE, BACON AND APPLE SALAD

SERVES 4

I cup blue brie, rind removed and diced
¼ lb bacon, rinds removed
I red-skinned apple, cored and chopped
I tablespoon lemon juice
⅓ cup hazelnuts, halved
½ cup sour cream

Place the cheese in a container. Broil the bacon and cut into small pieces. Mix with the cheese and add the apple, tossed in the lemon juice, the nuts and cream. Season with black pepper. Chill. Keep as cool as possible when transporting.

CŒUR À LA CRÈME

MAKES 8-12

Traditionally, heart-shaped china molds are used for this dessert.

2 cups cottage cheese
2 cups cream cheese
2 cups heavy cream, whipped
6 tablespoons superfine sugar
4 egg whites
TO SERVE
light cream
superfine sugar
fresh fruit

Press the cheeses through a fine nylon sieve. Gently fold in the cream and sugar. Beat the egg whites stiffly and fold in. Line the molds with pieces of scalded cheesecloth. Divide the mixture between the molds and stand them on plates to drain overnight in the refrigerator. Transport the creams in the molds. Unmold just before serving and peel away the cheesecloth. Serve the creams with cream, sugar and fresh fruit of the season – strawberries or raspberries are ideal.

SPECIAL SUMMER PUDDING

SERVES 6-8

1 8-in square pound cake
½ lb raspberries
½ lb redcurrants, stalks removed
½ lb strawberries, hulled
1 lemon, grated rind only
¾ cup red wine
2 tablespoons port
4 tablespoons superfine sugar

Cut the cake into 4 or 5 thin layers. Cut each layer into long thin triangles and use these to line a 3 pint pudding bowl or mold. Press any trimmings into the holes to make a complete lining of cake. Reserve enough cake to cover the top of the bowl.

Place the raspberries and redcurrants in a large bowl. Cut the strawberries in half and add them to the bowl with the lemon rind.

Pour the wine, port and sugar into another pan and heat gently until the sugar dissolves. Add the fruit and simmer for 5 minutes. Remove from the heat and cool slightly. Taste for sweetness and add a little more sugar if liked. Spoon the fruit and its juices into the prepared bowl or mold and cover with the reserved cake. Place a saucer on top and weight it. Chill overnight.

Transport the pudding in the bowl. Turn out just before serving. Serve with whipped cream.

FALL BOUNTY

The balmy days of fall are often warm enough to spend outside picnicking. With fruit and nuts growing ripe on the trees, it is also the time to go out gathering – so why not combine the two?

Serious fruit-pickers will have developed an appetite by lunchtime, so provide a selection of tempting dishes. Smoked Trout Baklava cut into diamond shapes. Ham and Cheese Croissants. Tiny Ricotta and Smoked Salmon Turnovers and Vegetable Crudités with Garlic and Walnut Dip would make a mouth-watering display.

Follow with fruit-laden desserts, perhaps an Open Cherry Pie and a Baked Plum Cheesecake. Then, for sustenance through the afternoon, hold back some Crunchy Caramel Cones and Coffee Brazil Snaps for good measure.

POTTED TONGUE

SERVES 6

1 cup sweet butter, melted
½ lb sliced tongue, chopped
pinch ground allspice
pinch ground nutmeg
1 tablespoon brandy

Allow the melted butter to stand so that the clear golden butter floats on the sediment of whey and salt. Spoon off the butter and discard the cloudy sediment. Pound or grind the tongue with two-thirds of the butter. Add the spices, brandy and plenty of freshly-ground black pepper. Press this mixture firmly into small pots and smooth the surface level. Pour the remaining clarified butter over the tongue and chill until set and sealed. Cover with foil to transport. Serve with crackers and water cress.

SMOKED TROUT BAKLAVA

MAKES ABOUT 30

1 bunch scallions, sliced
2 tablespoons butter
1 bunch water cress, trimmed and chopped
1-2 tablespoons creamed horseradish
4 smoked trout fillets, skinned and flaked
6 cups cottage cheese, sieved
12 sheets filo pastry
¼ cup butter, melted

Fry the scallions in the butter for 3 minutes. Remove from the heat and stir in the water cress. Mix the horseradish with the fish. Soften the cottage cheese and blend in the scallions and water cress. Stir in the fish mixture. Butter an 11-inch baking pan and cut six sheets of pastry to fit inside the pan. Butter each sheet in turn and place in the bottom of the pan. Spread the filling over this and cover with six more sheets of buttered pastry. Cut the top layer of pastry into small diamond shapes (about 30) and brush again with butter. Bake at 400°F for 35-40 minutes until golden. Cool in the pan for 20 minutes.

Cut the baklava into diamonds and cool on a wire rack. Pack, interleaved with waxed paper, in a rigid container.

HAM AND CHEESE CROISSANTS

MAKES 12

1 cake compressed yeast
1 cup lukewarm milk
¼ cup melted butter, cooled
1 egg, beaten
1 teaspoon salt
4 cups all-purpose flour
¾ cup butter blended with ¼ cup all-purpose flour
FILLING
2 slices ham, chopped
1 cup Gruyère cheese, grated
beaten egg, to glaze

Cream the yeast with the milk, add the melted butter, egg and salt. Pour into a well in the flour and mix to a smooth dough. Knead until smooth and elastic (about 10 minutes). Place in an oiled plastic bag and leave to rise in a warm place until doubled in size – about 1 hour.

Knead the dough lightly to remove the air and roll it out to a rectangle 8 by 18 inches. Have a short end nearest you. Dot a third of the blended butter and flour mixture over the top two thirds of the dough rectangle. Fold the bottom third of the dough up over the middle third and the top third down over that. Press the edges together with the rolling pin to seal. Turn the dough through 90° to the left. Return to the plastic bag and chill for 15 minutes. Repeat the process twice more using the remaining blended butter, then repeat the rolling and folding twice more without butter. Be sure to chill the dough between each process so that the fat does not melt. Finally cut the dough in half. Roll each piece evenly to a 24 by 8-inch strip. Cut the strips into 12 long triangles.

Mix the ham and cheese and divide into 12 portions. Place a portion at the wide end of each dough triangle. Roll up the triangles from the filled end to the tip. Curve into crescent shapes. Place on greased baking sheets. Cover with oiled plastic wrap and prove in a warm place for 30 minutes. Brush with beaten egg and bake at 425°F for 10 to 15 minutes. Wrap in paper toweling while still hot and transport in an insulated box to the picnic to be eaten while still warm.

CREAMY HAM CROUSTADES

MAKES 12

1 large loaf of white bread, unsliced with crusts removed
½ cup butter, melted
FILLING
¾ cup cream cheese
½ cup light cream
salt, freshly-ground black pepper
¾ cup cooked ham, chopped
2 tablespoons fresh chives, chopped
2 tablespoons pistachio nuts, chopped
2 teaspoons mild whole grain mustard
GARNISH
paprika
alfalfa sprouts

Cut the bread into slices 2-inches thick. Cut each slice into two 2-inch squares. Set the bread cubes on a baking sheet.

Cut into the cubes, ¼in from the edge and nearly through to the base to make box shapes, scooping out the crumb. Brush the boxes inside and out with the melted butter. Bake at 400°F for 15 to 20 minutes until golden and crisp. Allow to cool on a wire rack. To make the filling, blend the cream cheese and light cream. Add salt and freshly-ground black pepper. Stir in the ham, chives, nuts and mustard. Chill.

Just before packing, spoon the filling into the croustades and garnish each with a sprinkling of paprika and a few alfalfa sprouts. Pack into a rigid container and keep as cool as possible.

VARIATION   *Cheese and Mustard Cups*
Make as for the Creamy Ham Croustades but fill with a cheese and mustard mixture. Melt 2 tablespoons butter in a small pan. Stir in 1 tablespoon all-purpose flour and cook for 1 minute. Blend in 1 tablespoon mustard and ¾ cup milk and cook to a smooth sauce. Stir in ½ cup each of cream and a crumbly cheese and season with freshly-ground white pepper. Allow to cool.

VEGETABLE CRUDITÉS WITH GARLIC AND WALNUT DIP

SERVES 6

1 small cauliflower, broken into florets
1 green bell pepper, cored, deseeded and cut into
strips
2 red-skinned apples, cored, sliced and tossed in
lemon juice
3 sticks celery, trimmed, cut into sticks
3 carrots, cut into thin sticks
¼ cucumber, cut into thin sticks
DIP
¾ cup mayonnaise
¾ cup heavy cream, whipped
1 clove garlic, crushed in a little salt
4 tablespoons walnuts, finely-ground
1 teaspoon lemon juice
freshly-ground white pepper

Prepare the vegetables and fruit and sprinkle them with a few drops of water. Seal them in plastic bags and chill. Transport the vegetables and fruit in the bag. To make the dip fold the mayonnaise into the cream. Stir in the garlic, walnuts and lemon juice. Add plenty of freshly-ground white pepper. Chill in a sealed container and serve with the vegetables and fruit.

VARIATION   *Green Herb Dip*
Replace the garlic and walnuts with 2 tablespoons chopped water cress. 1 tablespoon fresh chopped parsley and 1 tablespoon fresh chopped chervil. Make the dip as described.

VEAL AND TONGUE TERRINE

SERVES 6-8

PASTRY
3 cups all-purpose flour
1 teaspoon allspice
¾ cup butter
1 egg, beaten
water to mix
FILLING
1 lb lean veal, cut into thick slices
1 lb cooked tongue, cut into thick slices
3 tablespoons fresh chopped parsley
1 tablespoon mint jelly
1 lemon, grated rind and juice
½ cup white wine
beaten egg, to glaze
TO FINISH
1 teaspoon unflavored gelatin

Sift the flour and allspice into a large bowl and rub in the butter. Add the egg and just enough cold water to bind to a dough. Knead lightly until smooth and use three quarters of the dough to line a 2 lb loaf pan. Combine all the ingredients for the filling in a large bowl. Cover and marinate for 2 hours. Drain the meat, reserving the marinade and spoon the meat into the prepared loaf pan. Use the remaining pastry to make a lid and use any trimming for decorations. Crimp and seal the crust and make a hole in the lid to allow the steam to escape. Brush with beaten egg. Bake at 425°F for 20 minutes. Reduce the heat to 350°F for 1½ hours.

Dissolve the gelatin in the reserved juice of the marinade and pour into the terrine as it cools. Pack the terrine in foil and serve in slices at the picnic or, alternatively, cut slices before leaving home and wrap individually.

TINY RICOTTA AND SMOKED SALMON TURNOVERS

MAKES 16

2 cups ricotta cheese
¾ cup smoked salmon trimmings, chopped
2 tablespoons fresh parsley, chopped
½ lemon, grated rind only
1-2 teaspoons pink peppercorns, drained
8 sheets filo pastry
6 tablespoons butter, melted

Blend the cheese with the salmon, parsley, lemon rind and peppercorns. Season to taste with freshly-ground black pepper. Divide this filling into 16 portions. Work with one sheet of pastry at a time and keep the rest under a damp cloth. Divide a sheet of pastry in half lengthways. Brush each half with butter and lay a portion of the filling at a short end of each. For each piece of pastry follow the same procedure: fold both long sides in towards the center, over the filling at one end. Roll the filled end along the strip to make a neat turnover. Brush with more butter and place on a baking sheet. Repeat with the remaining pastry and filling.

Bake the turnovers at 400°F for 10 to 12 minutes until golden brown and crispy. Cool on a wire rack. Pack the turnovers in a rigid container for transportation.

FRANGIPANE PIE

SERVES 6-8

1 quantity sweet shortcrust pastry (see Open Cherry
Pies, page 84)
½ cup good-quality raspberry jelly
FILLING
½ cup butter
½ cup superfine sugar
2 eggs, beaten
1 cup finely-ground almonds
1 tablespoon all-purpose flour
few drops almond extract
2 oz ready-made marzipan, coarsely grated

Roll out the pastry and use it to line a 9-inch pie
plate or dish. Spread the base of the pastry with
the jelly. To make the filling, cream the butter and
sugar together until light and fluffy. Gradually beat
in the eggs a little at a time. Fold in the ground
almonds, flour and extract. Spread the mixture in
the pastry case and set the dish on a baking sheet.
Bake at 375°F for 40-45 minutes until risen and
spongy. Scatter the marzipan over the pie and
return to the oven for 5 minutes. Cool. Transport
the pie in the dish. Serve sliced with slices of fresh
fruit.

HONEY AND WHITE RAISIN DROP BISCUITS

MAKES 18-20

2 cups self-rising flour
½ teaspoon baking powder
2 eggs, beaten
2 tablespoons butter, melted
3 tablespoons thick honey
1¼ cups milk
¼ cup white raisins
oil for cooking

Place the flour, baking powder, eggs, butter, honey
and milk in a blender or food processor and
blend until very smooth. Stir in the white raisins.
Heat a heavy-based skillet or griddle and brush
lightly with oil. Drop spoonfuls of the mixture on
to the griddle and cook over a medium heat until
bubbles appear on the surface. Turn the biscuits
over and cook the other side for 2 to 3 minutes.
Cool on a clean dish towel. Butter the biscuits and
pack in a rigid container or box, interleaved with
waxed paper.

PINE NUT SAVORY BREAD

MAKES 1 LARGE LOAF

1 cake compressed yeast
1¾ cups lukewarm milk
6 cups all-purpose flour
2 tablespoons salt
2 tablespoons sugar
2 tablespoons butter
½ lb smoked bacon
¼ cup pine nuts
milk, to glaze

Blend the yeast in the milk. Sift the flour, salt and sugar into a warmed bowl. Rub in the butter and pour in the yeast mixture. Mix to a smooth dough and knead for 10 minutes on a lightly-floured surface until soft and smooth. Place in an oiled plastic bag in a warm place and leave to rise until doubled in size.

Broil the bacon until crisp and chop.

Remove the dough from the bag and knead in the bacon and pine nuts. Cut the dough into 5 pieces and form each into a small roll. Cover with oiled plastic wrap and allow to prove until the dough reaches the top of the pan. Remove the film, brush with milk and bake at 450°F for 45 to 50 minutes. Cover the loaf with foil if it begins to brown too quickly. Allow to cool on a wire rack. Slice and butter the bread and pack in slices in a rigid container.

MARMALADE FRENCH APPLE PIE

SERVES 4-6

PASTRY
1½ cups all-purpose flour
½ cup butter
¼ cup confectioners' sugar
1 egg yolk
FILLING
3 cooking apples, peeled, cored and roughly chopped
3 tablespoons rough-cut marmalade
1 orange, finely-grated rind and juice
TOPPING
1 desert apple, quartered, cored and thinly sliced
3 tablespoons marmalade
1 tablespoon lemon juice

To make the pastry, sift the flour into a large bowl and rub in the butter until it resembles fine bread crumbs. Stir in the sugar and just enough egg yolk to make a firm dough. Chill for 30 minutes. Line a 9-inch pie pan or dish with the pastry. Chill again for 30 minutes then bake blind for 15 to 20 minutes until the crust is golden brown. Cool in the pan or dish. To make the filling, place all the ingredients plus 1 tablespoon of water into a tightly-lidded pan and heat gently until the apple is cooked to a pulp. Beat until smooth, then cool. Spread into the base of the pastry case.

To make the topping, arrange the apple slices over the surface of the filling. Place the marmalade and lemon juice in a small pan and bring to the boil. Press through a sieve and brush over the apple and crust of the pie. Transport in the pan. Serve with cream, or thick yogurt if liked.

COFFEE BRAZIL SNAPS

MAKES 20

¼ cup butter
1 cup all-purpose flour
4 tablespoons superfine sugar
½ cup Brazil nuts, finely ground
½ egg, beaten
FROSTING
¾ cup confectioners' sugar
1 teaspoon coffee extract
crushed coffee sugar crystals

Rub the butter into the flour. Stir in the sugar, nuts and egg and knead to a smooth dough. Shape into a 2-inch square-cornered 'sausage' and wrap in foil. Chill for 1 hour until firm.

With a sharp knife cut thin slices of dough. Place on greased baking sheets and chill for 30 minutes more. Bake at 400°F for 6 to 8 minutes. Allow to cool on the baking sheets for a few minutes then remove to a wire rack.

To make the frosting, blend together the confectioners' sugar, extract and just enough water to make a thick smooth mixture. Brush over the cookies and sprinkle with crushed sugar crystals. Allow to set.

Pack in a rigid container, interleaved with waxed paper.

OPEN CHERRY PIES

MAKES 14

SWEET SHORTCRUST PASTRY
2 cups all-purpose flour
½ cup butter
1 tablespoon superfine sugar
1 egg, beaten
FILLING
1 tablespoon ground almonds
1 lb fresh or bottled cherries, pitted (or use any soft fruit available)
½ to ¾ cup redcurrant jelly, warmed
DECORATION
mint sprigs

Sift the flour into a bowl. Rub in the butter finely. Stir the sugar into the egg until dissolved. Add just enough of the egg mixture to the flour to make a soft dough. Chill for 15 minutes then knead lightly. Roll out on a lightly-floured surface and cut out 3-inch rounds with a pastry cutter. Use the rounds to line muffin pans and prick each well with a fork. Chill for 30 minutes. Bake at 375°F for 10-15 minutes until just golden. Cool in the pans for 15 minutes then remove to a wire rack.

Sprinkle a little of the ground almonds in each pastry case. Fill with the pitted cherries or other fruit. Spoon or brush the jelly over the fruit to seal it. Decorate each with a sprig of mint.

Pack in a rigid container, interleaved with waxed paper. Keep chilled until ready to serve.

VARIATION   *Raspberry Tartlets*
Make as for the Open Cherry Pies but use fresh raspberries and top with raspberry jelly.

ALMOND MERINGUE SPHERES

MAKES 18

1 egg white
½ cup confectioners' sugar, sifted
FILLING
2 tablespoons sugar
2 tablespoons water
1 egg yolk
¼ cup sweet butter
few drops almond extract, or 1 teaspoon Amaretto
liqueur
1½ cups blanched almonds, finely chopped

Beat the egg white stiffly in a glass bowl. Set the bowl over a pan of simmering water. Add the sugar and beat continuously until the mixture is shiny and very stiff. Remove the bowl from the heat and beat until cool. Pipe or spoon the meringue into small round heaps on greased and lined baking sheets. Bake at 300°F for 1½ hours until crisp. Cool on wire racks.

For the filling, dissolve the sugar in the water in a small pan over gentle heat. Bring to the boil, without stirring and boil until the temperature reaches 230°F. Gradually beat the bubbling syrup into the egg yolk in a thin stream. Continue to beat until cool and thick. Gradually beat in pieces of softened butter until the mixture is thick and glossy. Finally beat in the almond extract or Amaretto. Use a little of the filling mixture to sandwich the meringue spheres together in pairs. Spread the remaining filling round the outside of the balls and roll them in the chopped almonds. Place each sphere in a small paper baking cup and pack in a rigid container.

PARIS BREST GÂTEAUX

SERVES 6

¾ cup water
¼ cup butter
½ cup, plus 2 teaspoons all-purpose flour, sifted
2 eggs, beaten
egg white, to glaze
¼ cup slivered almonds
FILLING
¼ cup whole blanched almonds
scant ¾ cup superfine sugar
1¼ cups milk
2 egg yolks
few drops of vanilla extract
1 tablespoon flour
½ cup heavy cream, whipped
DECORATION
confectioners' sugar

Place the water and butter in a small pan and heat gently until the butter melts. Bring to the boil and quickly add the flour all at once. Beat over the heat until the flour comes away from the sides of the pan and a smooth paste forms. Cook for 1 minute more. Cool slightly. Gradually beat in just enough of the egg to make a firm, smooth glossy paste. Using a large pastry bag and a ½-inch plain nozzle pipe the paste into 6 small rings on a greased baking sheet.

Bake at 425°F for 30 minutes then cool for 10 minutes. Brush with egg white and sprinkle with the nuts. Return to the oven for 5 minutes until crisp and browned. Cool on a wire rack.

To make the filling, place the blanched almonds and ⅓ cup of the superfine sugar in a heavy-based pan. Heat gently until the sugar melts. Stir briefly and pour on to an oiled baking sheet. Cool. Crush coarsely. Scald the milk. Beat the egg yolks, extract and remaining sugar together until thick and light. Stir in the flour. Beat in the milk and pour into a pan. Bring to the boil, beating all the time and cook for 2 minutes. Cover the surface with plastic wrap to prevent a skin forming and allow to cool.

Press the custard through a fine sieve, fold in the whipped cream and crushed sugar and nut mixture.

Split the choux rings just before packing and fill with the mixture. Dust with a little confectioners' sugar. Pack in a rigid container and keep cool.

CHOCOLATE CHIP MOUSSE

4 eggs, separated
¾ cup superfine sugar
¾ cup bitter chocolate, melted
3 tablespoons crème de cacao or brandy
½ oz unflavored gelatin, dissolved in 3 tablespoons
boiling water, cooled
I cup heavy cream
¼ cup white chocolate, chopped
DECORATION
light cream, chocolate curls

Beat the egg yolks with the superfine sugar until very thick and pale. Cool the melted chocolate and stir into the mixture with the liqueur or brandy. Stir in the dissolved gelatin. Whip the cream and fold in with the chopped chocolate. Pour the mousse into 6 or 8 individual pots and leave in a cool place to set. Transport in the pots. Serve with light cream and chocolate curls.

CRUNCHY CARAMEL CONES

MAKES 10-12

3 tablespoons superfine sugar
¼ cup butter
¼ cup light corn syrup
½ cup all-purpose flour, sifted
I teaspoon coriander seeds, roughly crushed
I tablespoon sesame seeds
I teaspoon lemon juice
¾ cup semisweet chocolate, melted

Place the sugar, butter and syrup in a small saucepan and melt over a gentle heat. Bring to the boil and remove from the heat. Stir in the flour, seeds and lemon juice. Drop small spoonfuls of the mixture well spaced on baking sheets lined with parchment paper. Bake, one sheet at a time, at 350°F for 8 to 10 minutes until golden brown round the edges.

Remove them from the paper with a palette knife and wrap each round an oiled cream horn mold to form a cone shape. When set (3-5 minutes), remove and cool on a wire rack. Dip the point of each cone into the chocolate and leave to cool until set.

Serve plain, or fill with sweetened whipped cream.

Pack the cones in a rigid container in one layer and keep cool and dry.

WHITE RAISIN STREUSEL CAKES

MAKES 16 PIECES

¾ cup butter, softened
1½ cups soft brown sugar
3 eggs, beaten
1½ cups self-rising flour
½ teaspoon ground mixed spice
½ cup white raisins
TOPPING
1 cup butter
1¼ cups all-purpose flour
½ cup ground hazelnuts
¾ cup soft light brown sugar

Put the butter, sugar, eggs, flour, spice and white raisins in a large bowl and beat well together for 3 minutes until smooth. Spread into a greased and lined 8-inch square pan.

To make the topping, rub the butter into the flour until the mixture resembles bread crumbs. Stir in the ground nuts and sugar. Sprinkle this crumble mixture over the cake mixture in the pan. Bake at 350°F for 45 to 50 minutes. Cool in the pan for 15 minutes. Cut into bars and cool on a wire rack.

Pack in a rigid container.

BAKED PLUM CHEESECAKE

SERVES 8

BASE
¼ cup butter, softened
3 tablespoons superfine sugar
1 egg, beaten
½ cup self-rising flour
2 teaspoons milk
FILLING
¾ lb ripe plums, pitted and quartered
1 cup cream cheese, softened
4 cups cottage cheese, sieved
3 tablespoons superfine sugar
2 eggs, beaten
¾ cup sour cream
DECORATION
fresh sliced plums

To make the base, beat together all the ingredients until smooth. Spread in a greased and lined 8-inch loose-based cake pan. Bake at 375°F for 20 minutes. Leave in the pan to cool.

To make the filling, arrange the plums over the cake base. Beat together the remaining filling ingredients until smooth. Carefully pour over the plums. Return to the oven at 350°F for 30 minutes until just set. Cool. Transport in the pan.

Just before serving remove the pan and paper and serve in slices with fresh plums and a little light cream if liked.

ROSE PETAL JELLY

MAKES 2 LB

2 lb cooking apples, washed and cut up roughly
about 2½ cups water
2 cups preserving sugar per 2½ cups of juice
petals from 3 freshly-picked pink roses
few drops rose water
few drops red food coloring, if liked

Place the apples in a large pan and pour in just enough water to cover. Bring to a simmer and cook for about 1 hour until soft and pulpy. Mash against the sides of the pan with a wooden spoon. Strain the fruit juice through a scalded jelly bag into a bowl. Do not squeeze the fruit but allow it to drop for at least 1 hour, or overnight.

Measure the strained juice into a clean pan. Bring to a slow simmer and add 2 cups sugar per 2½ cups of juice. Stir until the sugar has dissolved. Add three-quarters of the rose petals, bring to the boil and boil briskly until setting point is reached. Check for setting point by placing a teaspoonful of mixture on a chilled saucer. After one minute, if a finger pushed against the jelly causes the surface to wrinkle then setting point has been reached. Remove the pan from the heat. Skim off the scum and rose petals.

Add the rose water, coloring and remaining rose petals. Pour into small, clean, warm jars. Top immediately with paraffin and cover with plastic wrap. Allow to cool.

Transport rose petal jelly in a jar.

CREAMED CHOCOLATE DRINK

SERVES 6

4 cups milk
¾ cups heavy cream
1 cup semisweet chocolate, broken into pieces
TO SERVE
whipped cream
ground cinnamon

Place the milk, cream and chocolate in a pan and gently heat until evenly blended and just below simmering point. Pour into a thermos. Take a small container of whipped cream and float a little of this on each serving, dusted with cinnamon if liked.

NEW YEAR'S DAY

A frosty New Year's Day morning tempts post-Christmas revellers outside and provides another excuse for a sensational picnic. A selection of tantalizing snacks, hot soups and unusual casseroles should stir even the most sluggish appetites.

Spicy dishes like Cocktail Chicken Tandoori and Peppered Roast Beef make delicious starters. Serve them with hot Tomato Chowder to combat the cold. For a hearty main course, the Cassoulet Pot, which is full of chicken, vegetables, navy beans, smoked pork sausage and bacon, is ideal. If the weather is mild, a selection of salads might be appropriate. Unusual ones like Creamy Pesto Tagliatelle Salad and Pink Grapefruit and Avocado Salad could be served with the impressive-looking Nutty Bacon Braid.

For a festive dish with a difference, supply large quantities of Orange and Almond Fruit Pies served with lashings of brandied cream or Cointreau Butter.

CREAMY CHEESE RISOTTO

SERVES 4

I oz butter
I tablespoon olive oil
2 cups risotto rice
1 onion, finely chopped
3¾ cups chicken stock
3 oz Gruyère cheese, grated
3 oz Emmental cheese, grated
I tablespoon Parmesan cheese, grated
GARNISH
4 bacon slices, broiled crisp, crumbled

Melt the butter and oil in a large pan. Add the rice and onion and fry for 2 to 3 minutes. Pour in the stock, bring to the boil, stir and allow to simmer for 15 to 20 minutes until most of the stock has been absorbed but the rice is still creamy. Stir in the cheeses, season and heat through. Keep hot in a food thermos and serve hot, sprinkled with crumbled bacon and with a green salad.

CASSOULET POT

MAIN DISH   SERVES 6

½ lb navy beans, soaked overnight in cold water
2 carrots, peeled and chopped
2 onions, peeled and chopped
2 sticks celery, chopped
I bouquet garni
½ lb bacon, without rinds and chopped
I clove garlic, peeled and crushed
I 2½ lb chicken, jointed into 8 pieces
4 tablespoons tomato paste
2¾ cups chicken stock
¾ lb smoked pork sausage, sliced
4 tablespoons fresh parsley, chopped

Drain the beans and place in a large pan covered with fresh cold water. Bring to the boil and boil for 10 minutes. Reduce the heat to a simmer and add the carrots, onion, celery and bouquet garni. Season with freshly-ground black pepper, cover and simmer for I hour.

In another pan, fry the bacon in its own fat for 3 minutes. Add the garlic and cook for I minute. Add the chicken pieces and cook until the pieces are browned on all sides. Add the tomato paste and stock. Season and simmer for 40 minutes until the chicken is tender.

Remove the chicken skin and discard it. Cut the meat from the bones. Drain the beans and vegetables and place in an ovenproof casserole. Add the chicken meat. Skim the chicken cooking liquor and add to the pan with the bacon. Stir in the sausage and parsley. Bake at 350°F for I hour 15 minutes. Remove from the oven and wrap the casserole in towels and insulating bags. Serve hot at the picnic with baked potatoes, fresh from the oven, wrapped in foil and packed in a similar way to the cassoulet, and pieces of crusty bread.

TOMATO CHOWDER

SERVES 6

2 tablespoons oil
1 clove garlic, peeled and crushed
1 onion, finely chopped
2 sticks celery, thinly sliced
4 slices bacon, derinded, chopped
2½ cups potatoes, peeled and cubed
4 tablespoons tomato paste
4 tomatoes, skinned and chopped
sprig oregano
2 tablespoons fresh parsley, chopped
pinch of sugar
1 teaspoon Worcestershire sauce
4 cups chicken or vegetable stock
salt, freshly-ground black pepper

Heat the oil in a large pan and fry the garlic, onion, celery and bacon for 4 minutes. Stir in the potatoes and cook for 1 minute. Blend the tomato paste with the chopped tomatoes and herbs. Stir into the pan with the remaining ingredients. Season to taste with salt and freshly-ground black pepper. Simmer gently for about 10 minutes until the potatoes are tender.

Pour into a large thermos for transportation. Serve with whole wheat rolls and butter.

CHICKEN NOODLE SOUP

SERVES 4-6

2 tablespoons butter
1½ cups button mushrooms, sliced
1 onion, peeled and chopped
5 cups well-flavored, homemade chicken stock
2 cooked chicken quarters, skinned and boned
freshly-ground white pepper
½ cup vermicelli pasta
3 tablespoons fresh parsley, chopped

Heat the butter in a large pan. Fry the mushrooms and onion for 4 minutes. Add the stock and the chicken, torn into small pieces. Bring to the boil. Skim any fat from the surface. Season with freshly-ground white pepper and add the pasta. Simmer for 10 minutes. Stir in the parsley and pour into a thermos for transportation.

CALZONE

SERVES 4-6

½ oz fresh yeast
1¼ cups lukewarm water
pinch of salt
pinch of sugar
3 cups of all-purpose flour
1 tablespoon olive oil
FILLING
1½ cups ricotta cheese
1½ cups mozzarella cheese, grated
6 oz salami, shredded
3 tablespoons fresh Parmesan cheese, grated
3 eggs, beaten
salt, pepper

Dissolve the yeast in the water and stir in the salt and sugar. Pour the mixture into the flour with the oil and mix to a dough. Knead until smooth and elastic – about 10 minutes. Cover with clear plastic wrap and leave to rise in a warm place until doubled in size.

To make the filling, mix the ingredients together, reserving 1 tablespoon of beaten egg for glazing. Add plenty of seasoning. Knock back the risen dough and divide into 6 pieces. Roll a piece of dough out thinly on a lightly-floured surface to make an 8-inch circle. Place one-sixth of the filling on the dough and wet the edges of the circle. Fold one side of the dough over to make a semi-circle shape and seal the edges. Place on a baking sheet and brush with a little egg yolk. Repeat with the remaining dough and filling. Bake at 450°F for 10 to 15 minutes. Allow to cool, or keep warm and serve hot at the picnic.

MUSTARD HAM IN PASTRY

MAIN DISH   SERVES 10-12

6 lb piece boneless, cooked ham
4 tablespoons whole grain mustard
2 tablespoons redcurrant jelly
3 tablespoons fresh parsley, chopped
PASTRY
½ cup butter
½ cup shortening
pinch of salt
pinch of ground allspice
4 cups all-purpose flour
iced water to mix
1 egg, beaten with a pinch of salt

Trim any fat from the meat. In a small bowl blend the mustard, jelly and parsley. Spread this evenly over the meat surface and leave it to stand. Make the pastry by rubbing the butter and shortening into the salt, spices and flour. When the mixture resembles fine bread crumbs stir in just enough water to mix to a firm dough. Roll out the pastry thinly on a lightly-floured surface. Have it just large enough to enclose the meat. Place the meat in the center of the pastry and bring up the sides of the pastry to make a neat turnover. Seal the joins with beaten egg and place the turnover with joins underneath on a greased baking sheet. Use the pastry trimmings to make leaves and flowers to decorate the turnover. Brush with beaten egg and chill for 30 minutes.

Bake at 400°F for about 40 minutes until crisp and golden brown. Cool on a wire rack. Wrap in foil and transport whole. Carve in slices at the picnic. Serve with pickles and salad. Alternatively, carve the ham at home and wrap portions individually.

COCKTAIL CHICKEN TANDOORI

MAIN DISH   SERVES 6-8

6 chicken breasts, skinned, boned and cut into
chunks
2 tablespoons lime or lemon juice
1 teaspoon salt
1 tablespoon oil
2 teaspoons ground cardamom
2 teaspoons ground cumin
1 teaspoon mild ground chili
1 inch piece fresh green ginger, peeled and
shredded
2 cloves garlic, peeled and crushed
¾ cup unflavored yogurt
2 tablespoons butter

Place the chicken in a large shallow bowl. Sprinkle the juice and salt over the chicken and mix it in well. Heat the oil in a skillet and add the spices, ginger and garlic. Cook, stirring for 3 minutes. Remove the pan from the heat and stir in the yogurt. Pour the mixture over the chicken and cover. Marinate in the refrigerator overnight. The following day, arrange the chicken pieces and marinade in a large roasting pan. Dot with the butter and cook at 425°F for about 30 minutes or until tender. Baste occasionally during cooking.

Cool and pack in rigid containers. Serve on toothpicks.

NUTTY BACON BRAID

MAIN DISH   SERVES 6-8

1 onion, peeled and chopped
½ lb bacon, without rinds and chopped
¼ cup hazelnuts, chopped
2 carrots, peeled and grated
1 cup fresh bread crumbs
2 tablespoons fresh chopped parsley
freshly-ground coriander
1 lb shortcrust pastry
1 egg, beaten
poppy seeds

Place the onion, bacon, nuts, carrots, bread crumbs, parsley, seasoning and plenty of coriander in a large bowl and knead together. Form into an 8-inch long roll. Chill until firm. Roll out the pastry on a lightly-floured surface to an 8 by 12-inch rectangle. Place the bacon roll along the center of the pastry. Cut the exposed pastry into strips, leaving them attached at the center. Fold the strips, from alternate sides, over the bacon roll making a braid effect. Place the braid on an oiled baking sheet. Brush all over with beaten egg and sprinkle with poppy seeds. Bake at 425°F for 15 minutes. Reduce the temperature to 350°F for a further 40 minutes. Cool on a wire rack. Transport whole in a rigid container and serve cut in thick slices with salad. Alternatively, slice at home and put pieces on serving plates, covered with plastic wrap.

BEEF PASTRY TURNOVERS

MAIN DISH   MAKES 12

6 thin slices of beef round roast
¼ cup butter
1 small onion, finely chopped
1 clove garlic, peeled and crushed
1 egg, beaten
¼ cup fresh bread crumbs
6 tablespoons fresh herbs, (parsley, thyme, sage,
mint), chopped
1 lemon, finely-grated rind
oil for shallow frying
hot beef stock
1 bouquet garni
¾ cup red wine
1½ lb puff pastry
1 egg, beaten to glaze

Spread out the pieces of meat. Melt the butter in a pan and fry the onion and garlic for 4 minutes. Transfer to a small bowl and mix in the egg, bread crumbs, herbs and lemon rind. Divide the mixture between the slices of beef and spread it out over them. Season with freshly-ground black pepper. Roll up each slice like a jelly roll. Cut each roll into two to give 12 small rolls. Secure each with string or toothpicks.

Heat the oil in a flameproof casserole and fry the rolls until browned on all sides. Add just enough stock to cover and add the bouquet garni and red wine. Cover and cook at 350°F for 1¼ hours. Allow to cool in the stock. Drain the rolls and remove the string or tooth picks.

Roll out the pastry thinly and cut out 12 rectangles. Enclose each beef roll in a piece of pastry, brushing the edges of the pastry with egg to seal. Cut the pastry trimmings into long thin strips and use these to decorate the turnovers. Place the turnovers, joins underneath, on baking sheets and brush all over with beaten egg. Bake at 425°F for 15 to 20 minutes. Cool on a wire rack.

Pack in a rigid container and serve with whole grain mustard or horseradish relish.

PEPPERED ROAST BEEF

MAIN DISH   SERVES 8

3 lb boneless beef round roast, rolled and tied
1 tablespoon white peppercorns
1 tablespoon black peppercorns
1 tablespoon coriander seeds
1 clove garlic, peeled and crushed
3 tablespoons olive oil

Wipe the beef with paper toweling and stand it in a roasting pan. Crush the peppercorns and coriander seeds in a mortar and pestle or use a rolling pin on a chopping board. Mix with the garlic and spread all over the surface of the meat. Cover and leave to marinate for 2 to 3 hours. Pour the oil over the meat and roast at 450°F for 15 minutes then reduce the heat to 375°F for about 45 minutes for medium rare meat. Cool on a wire rack.

Carve thinly just before packing into an airtight shallow, rigid container.

CREAMY PESTO TAGLIATELLE SALAD

SERVES 6-8

1 cup uncooked tagliatelle
2 cloves garlic, peeled and chopped
½ cup pine nuts
3 tablespoons fresh basil leaves or parsley, chopped
¼ cup Parmesan cheese, freshly grated
4 tablespoons olive oil
freshly-ground black pepper
¾ cup sour cream
6 tablespoons unflavored yogurt

Cook the tagliatelle in plenty of salted boiling water until just tender. Drain, rinse in cold water, drain again and cool.

Place the garlic, pine nuts and herbs in a blender. Stir in the cheese and gradually stir in the oil. Season with freshly-ground black pepper. Stir in the sour cream and yogurt. Pour over the pasta and toss to coat evenly. Transport in a rigid container and keep cool. Serve with hot rolls.

PINK GRAPEFRUIT AND AVOCADO SALAD

SERVES 6

2 pink grapefruit
1 orange
1 cup smoked cheese
1 large avocado
¼ small head Chinese leaves, shredded
¼ cup walnuts, coarsely chopped

Peel the citrus fruit and remove all the pith. Cut the fruit into segments, catching the juice in a small bowl. Cut the cheese into thin sticks. Peel and pit the avocado. Cut it into slices and dip them in the collected fruit juice to prevent discoloration. Mix together the citrus fruits and any remaining juice, the cheese, avocado, Chinese leaves and walnuts. Chill and transport in a sealed container. Keep the salad cold.

GREEN BEANS VINAIGRETTE

SERVES 6-8

1 lb green beans, trimmed
DRESSING
6 tablespoons olive oil
2 tablespoons white wine vinegar
pinch of sugar
pinch of dry mustard
1 tablespoon fresh chopped parsley
1 hard-cooked egg, shelled

Cook the beans in boiling water until tender but still crisp. Drain.

Beat together the dressing ingredients, except the egg, and pour over the beans while they are still hot. Allow to cool in the dressing, turning them occasionally to coat them. Pack into a shallow container.

Separate the egg yolk from the white. Finely chop the egg white and press the yolk through a sieve. Sprinkle the egg over the beans. Seal and chill before transporting.

ORANGE AND ALMOND FRUIT PIES WITH COINTREAU BUTTER

MAKES 18

PASTRY
2 cups all-purpose flour
½ cup ground almonds
¼ cup confectioners' sugar, sifted
I orange, finely-grated rind
¾ cup butter
I egg yolk
¼ cup blanched almonds, chopped
½ jar fruit mincemeat
I egg white
superfine sugar
COINTREAU BUTTER
6 tablespoons butter
½ cup confectioners' sugar, sifted
2 tablespoons superfine sugar
3-4 tablespoons Cointreau

To make the pastry, mix the flour, almonds, sugar and orange peel in a large bowl. Rub in the butter and stir in the egg yolk to make a firm dough. Add a very little water if necessary. Knead lightly until smooth. Wrap in plastic and chill for 20 minutes.

Mix the chopped almonds with the mincemeat. Roll the dough out thinly, cut out about 18 rounds and use these to line muffin pans. Place a spoonful of mincemeat in each pastry shell. From the re-rolled pastry trimmings stamp out small stars using a cookie cutter. Place a star on the center of the mincemeat in each pie. Brush each with a little egg white and sprinkle with superfine sugar. Bake at 375°F for 12-15 minutes until golden brown. Cool on a wire rack or, for hot pies, pack them into a container immediately, interleaved with paper towelling. Wrap the container in a towel, then put it into an insulated bag. Serve with Cointreau Butter. For the butter: cream the butter and sugars until very light and fluffy. Gradually beat in the Cointreau drop by drop until it is absorbed. Pack into a small container and serve with the mincemeat pies.

TIPSY WINTER FRUIT SALAD

½ lb mixed dried fruits (apricots, pears, peaches and apples)
I lemon, grated rind and juice
I orange, grated rind and juice
5 cups strongly-made black tea
I cinnamon stick
¼ cup rum or sherry
sugar to taste

Place the dried fruit in a large bowl, add the fruit rinds and juices and pour over the tea. Leave to soak overnight. Next day, add the cinnamon stick and simmer gently for 20-30 minutes until the fruit is soft and tender. Stir in the rum or sherry, remove the cinnamon stick and then add sugar to taste. Serve chilled with unflavored yogurt.

RUM BABAS

MAKES 8

1 tablespoon superfine sugar
4 tablespoons lukewarm milk
2 teaspoons dry yeast
1 cup all-purpose flour
pinch of salt
2 eggs, beaten
¼ cup butter, melted
¾ cup currants
RUM SYRUP
¾ cup water
⅓ cup sugar
1 teaspoon lemon juice
4 tablespoons rum
TO DECORATE
6 tablespoons apricot jelly, warmed and sieved
sweetened whipped cream, to serve

Dissolve a pinch of the sugar in the milk in a pitcher and sprinkle the dry yeast over it. Beat with a fork for a few seconds. Leave in a warm place for 15 minutes until the mixture is very frothy. Sift the flour and salt into a large warmed bowl. Pour the yeast liquid into the flour. Beat the remaining sugar with the eggs and pour into the flour with the melted butter. Mix to gradually incorporate the flour. Beat for 2 minutes until a smooth batter is formed. Cover and leave to rest for 10 minutes. Beat the dough thoroughly for 5 minutes. Beat in the currants. Lightly grease 8 baba pans or dariole molds. Pour the dough into the pans and set them on a baking sheet. Cover with oiled plastic wrap. Leave to rise in a warm place for 30 to 40 minutes until the dough reaches the top of the tins. Bake at 450°F for 4 to 5 minutes then lower the temperature to 350°F for 5 minutes more. Turn out the babas, clean the pan with paper toweling and return the babas to their pans ready for soaking with syrup.

To make the syrup, place the water, sugar and lemon juice in a small pan and heat gently until dissolved. Bring to the boil for 10 minutes. Cool for 5 minutes. Stir in the rum. Prick the babas all over with a skewer. Pour the syrup over them in their pans. Let the syrup soak in and leave until completely cooled. Turn out and brush with jam.

Pack in a rigid container and serve with sweetened whipped cream and a little fresh fruit if liked.

SNOWY CHOCOLATE TRUFFLES

MAKES APPROXIMATELY 12-16

6 tablespoons sweet butter
1 cup confectioners' sugar, sifted
1⅓ cups white chocolate, very gently melted (see page 41)
1 tablespoon brandy
DECORATION
ground almonds

Beat the butter and confectioners' sugar together until creamy. Stir in the chocolate and brandy. Stir until thick and cooled. Chill until firm. Shape into walnut-sized balls. Roll in ground almonds. Chill before packing in a rigid container or small basket.

CARAMEL ALMOND PIE

SERVES 6-8

PASTRY
¾ cup all-purpose flour, sifted
1 tablespoon superfine sugar
1 cup butter
3-4 tablespoons water
FILLING
3 cups slivered almonds
¾ cup heavy cream
¾ cup sugar
few drops almond extract
1 orange, finely grated rind
1 tablespoon orange juice

To make the pastry, sift together the flour and sugar. Rub in the butter finely. Mix to a firm dough with the water. Wrap in plastic and chill for 30 minutes. Roll out on a lightly-floured surface and use to line an 8-inch quiche pan. Chill again for 30 minutes. Bake the pastry blind at 375°F for 15 to 20 minutes.

To make the filling, place all the ingredients in a pan and bring to the boil. Turn down the heat and simmer very gently, stirring constantly, for 10 to 15 minutes until the sugar dissolves. Pour into the pastry case and bake for a further 20 to 25 minutes until set. Allow to cool and transport in the pan. Serve cut into slices.

STOLLEN

SERVES 8

4 cups all-purpose flour
1 teaspoon salt
1 package easy-blend dry yeast
⅓ cup superfine sugar
½ cup butter, melted
1¼ cups lukewarm milk
2 eggs, beaten
½ lemon, grated rind only
1 cup blanched almonds, chopped
½ cup candied cherries, chopped
¾ cup candied peel
1 cup white raisins
TO DECORATE
confectioners' sugar
ribbon

Sift the flour and salt into a large warmed bowl. Stir in the yeast and sugar. Blend the melted butter with the milk and eggs and pour into the flour. Mix to a dough and turn out on to a lightly-floured surface. Knead for 10 minutes until the dough is soft and no longer sticky. Place in an oiled plastic bag and allow to rise in a warm place for 1 hour until doubled in size. Knock back the dough and knead in the remaining ingredients. Shape the dough into a large flat oval and fold one side over the other lengthways. Place on a greased baking sheet and cover with oiled plastic wrap. Leave to prove in a warm place for another hour. Remove the plastic wrap and bake at 400°F for about 45 minutes until the loaf is golden brown and sounds hollow when tapped underneath. Allow to cool on a wire rack.

Dust with confectioners' sugar and, for a festive look, tie with ribbon. Wrap in foil to transport and serve in slices.

VARIATION Make individual stollen by shaping the dough into rings or braids and tying a name to each baked cake with ribbon.

ST CLEMENT'S MERINGUE PIE

SERVES 4-6

¼ lb shortcrust pastry
FILLING
3 oz superfine sugar
1¼ cups water
1 lemon, grated rind and juice
1 orange, grated rind and juice
½ cup cornstarch
3 egg yolks
TOPPING
3 egg whites
½ cup plus 3 tablespoons superfine sugar

Line an 8-inch fluted pie pan with the pastry. Bake blind at 375°F for 15-20 minutes. Allow to cool. To make the filling, dissolve the sugar in the water in a small pan. Add the grated rinds and boil for five minutes. Blend the cornstarch with the fruit juices and pour the sugar syrup on to the cornstarch mixture. Return to the pan and cook gently, stirring until thickened. Remove from the heat and stir in the egg yolks. Spread the filling on the prepared pastry case.

To make the topping, beat the egg whites until very stiff. Beat in half the sugar then beat until stiff again. Fold in the remaining sugar. Pipe or pile on top of the filling. Bake at 350°F for 30 minutes until the top is just colored. Cool and transport in the pie pan. Serve with cream.

HOT SPICED MULL

SERVES 6-8

3 teaspoons superfine sugar
1 bottle dry red wine
1 cinnamon stick
5 coriander seeds
6 cloves
thinly-pared rind of ½ orange
thinly-pared rind of ½ lemon
1 tablespoon orange curaçao or brandy

Mix the sugar, wine, cinnamon, coriander, cloves and citrus rind in a large pan. Heat gently until the sugar dissolves and the mixture is just below simmering point. Add the liqueur or brandy and pour into a thermos. To serve, strain into glasses.

VARIATION   *Cider Glow*
Make as for the Hot Spiced Mull but replace the wine with a bottle of hard cider. Replace the curaçao with Calvados (apple brandy).

HONEY GLOGG

SERVES 8

⅓ cup seedless raisins
I teaspoon ground cloves
I teaspoon ground cinnamon
I teaspoon ground cardamom
8 tablespoons clear honey
I bottle dry red wine
¾ cup brandy

Place all the ingredients except the brandy in a large pan. Cover and heat very gently for about I hour to allow the flavors to mingle. Remove from the heat and pour in the brandy. Pour into a thermos and serve in small cups.

SPRING EXCURSION

The first signs of spring herald the start of the summer picnic season, and what better way to celebrate than with a picnic of gargantuan proportions. The food should reflect the creative extravagance of the natural world – this is no time to be reticent.

Soup is still a welcome sight at this time of the year, and Tropical Lentil Soup is wholesome and exotic. Serve it with a variety of starters: Brandied Liver Pâté with crackers and celery; Bacon and Pine Nut Filo Wheels; and Chili Shrimp and Avocado Cream. Warming casseroles can be transported to the picnic in a wide-necked thermos; provide a choice so that guests can try a bit of each. Rich Beef and Beet Hotpot is served with Mushroom and Parsley Pilau while the Orchard Pork Casserole goes well with whole wheat rolls and butter. Puff Top Chicken and Walnut Pies are best eaten hot as an accompaniment, or alternative to the casseroles.

For a festive touch, present an Easter Braid Garland surrounded by Marbled Chocolate Eggs and a selection of desserts, to finish.

BRANDIED LIVER-PÂTÉ

APPETIZER   SERVES 4-6

1 lb chicken livers
¼ teaspoon salt
pinch freshly-grated nutmeg
pinch ground cloves
pinch ground cinnamon
½ teaspoon dried mixed herbs
1 clove garlic, peeled and crushed
¼ cup brandy
1 cup butter
3 tablespoons heavy cream
GARNISH
½ cup sweet butter, clarified

Trim any stringy membranes from the livers and place in a shallow dish with the salt, spices, herbs, garlic and brandy. Cover and leave to marinate for several hours. Melt the butter in a large heavy skillet. Drain the livers and reserve the marinade juices. Add the livers to the butter and fry for 3 to 4 minutes, until firm but still pink in the center. Remove the livers and place in a food processor or blender. Pour the marinade juices into the butter in the pan and cook for 2 minutes. Pour the contents of the pan over the livers and blend to a purée. Stir in the cream and pour the paté into small pots. Chill until set. Finish with a layer of clarified butter on top of each pot to seal.

Transport in the pots and serve with crackers and celery.

BACON AND PINE NUT FILO WHEELS

APPETIZER   SERVES 6-8

½ lb bacon, derinded and chopped
2 tablespoons butter
I onion, peeled and chopped
I carrot, peeled and finely chopped
I cup fresh bread crumbs
I cup pine nuts
2 tablespoons fresh chopped parsley
I egg, beaten
8 sheets filo pastry
6 tablespoons melted butter

Fry the bacon in the butter for I minute. Add the vegetables and fry for 5 minutes until soft. Remove from the heat. Stir in the bread crumbs, pine nuts and parsley. Season with freshly-ground black pepper. Bind together with the egg.

Have the sheets of pastry in a stack and fold in half to form a 'book'. Brush each sheet of pastry with melted butter, gently turning the 'pages' as you go. Lay the pastry pile open flat and spread the bread crumb mixture over the top sheet, leaving 2 inches clear at one short side. Roll up all 8 sheets together from the opposite side finishing with the join underneath. Chill the roll for 30 minutes.

Cut the roll into ¾-inch slices and place them on a baking sheet. Brush the slices with any remaining melted butter and bake at 375°F for 30 minutes. Cool on a wire rack.

Pack in a rigid container.

CHILI SHRIMP AND AVOCADO CREAM

APPETIZER   SERVES 4-6

¾ lb large shelled shrimp
2 tablespoons olive oil
I clove garlic, peeled and crushed
pinch chili powder
I teaspoon soy sauce
few drops Tabasco sauce
freshly-ground black pepper
AVOCADO CREAM
I avocado
2 tablespoons lemon juice
¾ cup cottage cheese, sieved
½ red bell pepper, cored, deseeded and finely chopped

Thread the shrimp, 3 together on to toothpicks. Blend together the oil, garlic, chili, soy and Tabasco sauce and plenty of freshly-ground black pepper. Place the mixture in a large shallow container and add the skewered shrimp. Chill and marinate for several hours.

To make the Avocado Cream, peel and pit the avocado and mash the flesh with the lemon juice and cottage cheese until smooth.

Stir in the red bell pepper and season to taste. Pack the cream into a small sealed container and chill. Cover the marinade dish with the shrimp and marinade in it and drain just before serving with the cream dip.

TROPICAL LENTIL SOUP

SERVES 6

¾ cup split red lentils
2 tablespoons oil
1 onion, peeled and chopped
2 carrots, peeled and chopped
2 sticks celery, trimmed and chopped
3 slices bacon, rinds removed and chopped
1 green bell pepper, cored, deseeded and chopped
1 teaspoon whole grain mustard
1 teaspoon *garam marsala*
¼ cup creamed coconut
4 cups stock
1 tablespoon tomato paste
freshly-ground black pepper
TO SERVE
fresh cream

Soak the lentils in boiling water for 10 minutes. Drain. Heat the oil in a large pan and fry the onion, carrot, celery, bacon and pepper for 5 minutes. Add the mustard, *garam marsala* and lentils and cook for 2 minutes. Stir in the coconut, stock and tomato paste. Season with freshly-ground black pepper. Bring to the boil, cover and simmer for 50 minutes. Purée the soup in a blender or food processor until almost smooth. Transport in a thermos and serve hot with a little cream spooned on top.

MUSHROOM AND PARSLEY PILAU

MAIN DISH   SERVES 4-6

¼ cup butter
1 bunch scallions, trimmed and chopped
1 cup long-grain rice or risotto rice
2¼ cups button mushrooms, sliced
3½ cups chicken stock
6 tablespoons fresh parsley, chopped
¼ cup Parmesan cheese, freshly-grated
pinch freshly-grated nutmeg

Melt the butter in a large shallow pan. Add the scallions and rice and cook for 3 to 4 minutes without coloring. Stir in the mushrooms and stock and season with plenty of freshly-ground black pepper. Bring to the boil. Cover and simmer for about 30 minutes or until the rice is tender and the liquid is nearly absorbed. Stir in the parsley, cheese and nutmeg.

Place in a wide-necked thermos for transporting to the picnic.

VARIATION   *Mushroom Rice Salad*
Make as for the Mushroom and Parsley Pilau. Allow the mixture to cool when cooked. Stir through 2 tablespoons viniagrette dressing before serving.

PUFF TOP CHICKEN AND WALNUT PIES

MAIN DISH   MAKES 6

2 tablespoons oil
4 large chicken pieces
1 leek, trimmed and sliced
1 onion, peeled and sliced
1¼ cups chicken stock
salt, freshly-ground white pepper
2 tablespoons butter
1 tablespoon flour
¾ cup light cream
¾ cup walnuts, broken into pieces
PASTRY
3 cups all-purpose flour
pinch salt
pinch dry mustard
6 tablespoons butter
6 tablespoons shortening
iced water to mix
½ lb puff pastry
beaten egg, to glaze

Heat the oil in a flameproof casserole. Add the chicken pieces and fry briskly until browned on all sides. Add the leek and onion and fry for 1 minute. Pour in the stock and season. Cover and cook for 1 hour, simmering gently, until tender. Cool. Remove the skin and bones from the chicken. Tear the meat into small pieces and set aside with the strained vegetables. Reserve the stock.

Melt the butter in a small pan and add the flour. Cook for 2 minutes. Stir in 6 tablespoons of the reserved chicken stock and blend in the cream. Beat until smooth and cook for 3 minutes. Season with freshly-ground white pepper. Cool. Stir in the chicken meat and vegetables and add the walnuts.

To make the pastry, sift the flour, salt and mustard into a bowl. Rub in the butter and shortening and stir in just enough iced water to mix to a firm dough. Roll out and use to line 6 custard cups. Divide the creamed chicken filling between the pies. Roll out the puff pastry and cut out 6 rounds to make lids for the pies. Dampen the edges of the pastry and press on the lids. From the remaining puff pastry cut out decorations and attach to the lids with beaten egg. Cut a slit in each to allow the steam to escape and brush all over with beaten egg. Place the pies on a baking sheet and bake at 425°F for 15 minutes then reduce the heat to 375°F for a further 15 minutes. Cover with foil if the tops begin to over brown.

To eat hot at the picnic pack the custard cups into a large cookie container lined with dish towels. Wrap the container in more towels and place in an insulated bag. Serve hot, removing the pies from the custard cups just before serving.

ORCHARD PORK CASSEROLE

MAIN DISH   SERVES 6-8

3 green-skinned dessert apples
1 lb ripe pears
1 red-skinned dessert apple
1 lemon, grated rind and juice
2 lb pork tenderloin, cubed
¼ cup butter
2 onions, peeled and sliced
1 cup smoked pork sausage, sliced
2¾ cups stock
1 tablespoon fresh parsley, chopped
1 tablespoon fresh sage, chopped

Peel, core and slice the fruit and toss in the lemon rind and juice. Fry the pork in the butter in a flameproof casserole until browned on all sides. Add the onions and fry for 3 minutes. Stir in the sausage and stock and season with freshly-ground black pepper. Cover and cook for 1 hour over a very gentle heat. Add the herbs and fruit and continue to cook for another 40 minutes.

Transport in a wide-necked thermos and serve hot with whole wheat rolls and butter.

RICH BEEF AND BEET HOTPOT

MAIN DISH   SERVES 4-6

2 lb beef round steak
4 tablespoons oil
1 large onion, peeled and sliced
3 sticks celery, sliced
4½ cups flat mushrooms, sliced
2 teaspoons fresh horseradish, grated
1 teaspoon whole grain mustard
freshly-ground black pepper
1 lb raw beets, peeled and sliced
1¼ cups red wine or stock

Trim the beef and cut it into large cubes or strips. Heat the oil in a large flameproof casserole until it is very hot and fry the beef, in batches, to seal it. Remove the meat from the casserole. Fry the onion and celery for 3 minutes, add the mushrooms and fry for a further 3 minutes. Return the meat to the casserole and stir in the horse-radish, mustard and plenty of freshly-ground black pepper. Stir in the beets and red wine (or stock) and cover. Cook at 300°F for 3-4 hours until very tender. Pour into a wide-necked thermos for transportation and seal.

Serve with Mushroom and Parsley Pilau (page 108).

POTATO CHESTNUT CASSEROLE

MAIN DISH   SERVES 6

1 lb chestnuts
1½ lb potatoes, peeled and cut into cubes
¾ cup milk
¾ cup light cream
pinch freshly-grated nutmeg
salt, freshly-ground black pepper
¼ cup Gruyère cheese, grated

Make a deep slit in the skin of each chestnut. Place them in a roasting pan with 1¼ cups water and bake at 400°F for 10 to 15 minutes until the skins burst open. Allow to cool slightly. Remove the outer shells and the inner brown skin. Mix the potatoes and chestnuts in a casserole dish. Heat the milk and cream together to just below boiling point. Stir in the nutmeg, salt and freshly-ground black pepper. Pour over the potatoes and chest-nuts and sprinkle with the cheese. Cover and cook in a 400°F oven as above for 45 minutes. Remove the lid and cook for a further 15 minutes until the top has browned.

To transport and eat hot at the picnic, cover the casserole with the lid and wrap it in towels or a blanket, then put the whole package in an insul-ated bag. Serve with the Puff Top Chicken and Walnut Pies (page 109).

PORK, APPLE AND JUNIPER PIE

SERVES 4-6

2 tablespoons butter
2 tablespoons oil
1½ lb pork tenderloin, trimmed and cubed
1 leek, trimmed and sliced
1 onion, sliced
8 juniper berries, crushed
2 tablespoons tomato paste
1¼ cups stock
1 bouquet garni
3 dessert apples, peeled, cored and cubed
PASTRY
1½ lb all-purpose flour
2 teaspoons salt
½ cup shortening
¼ cup butter
1¼ cups water
1 egg, beaten
1 teaspoon unflavored gelatin

To make the filling, heat the butter and oil in a flameproof casserole. Fry the pork until browned on all sides. Add the leek and onion and fry for 5 minutes. Stir in the remaining ingredients except the apples. Simmer the casserole for 1 hour, add the apples and cook for a further 20 minutes. Drain off the stock and reserve. Cool the filling.

To make the pastry, sift the flour and salt into a large mixing bowl. Make a well in the center. Place the shortening, butter and water in a small pan. Heat until melted then bring to the boil. Pour into the flour and quickly mix to a fairly soft dough. Turn out on to a lightly-floured surface and knead until smooth. Reserve one quarter of the pastry. Use the remaining pastry to line the base and sides of a large raised pie mold or cake pan.

Spoon the prepared filling into the case and level the top. Roll out the reserved pastry and use to cover the pie and make a top. Dampen the edges of the crusts to seal. Trim, crimp the crusts and decorate with the trimmings. Make a ½-inch hole in the center of the top. Brush the top of the pie with beaten egg and bake at 400°F for 30 minutes. Brush again with beaten egg and reduce the oven temperature to 325°F for 45 minutes until golden brown. Dissolve the gelatin in the reserved stock and as the pie cools, pour it through the hole in the lid. Chill overnight. Transport in the pan and turn out before serving.

COFFEE CHOUX PUFFS

MAKES 10-12

¼ cup butter
¾ cup water
½ cup, plus 2 teaspoons all-purpose flour
2 eggs, beaten
FILLING
1¼ cups heavy cream
few drops vanilla extract
2 tablespoons superfine sugar
FROSTING
1 cup confectioners' sugar
1 teaspoon coffee extract
2 tablespoons crushed almonds

Place the butter and water in a small pan. Heat gently until the butter melts and bring to the boil. Add the flour all at once and beat, over the heat for 2 minutes until the mixture comes away from the sides of the pan. Allow to cool slightly. Gradually beat in the eggs, adding just enough to give a fairly stiff, smooth glossy paste. Place in a large pastry bag fitted with a plain nozzle and pipe rounds the size of ping-pong balls on to greased baking sheets. Bake at 425°F for 20 to 25 minutes until very crisp and light. Cool on a wire rack.

To make the filling, whip the cream, vanilla and sugar until it stands in peaks. Split the puffs and fill them with the cream.

To make the frosting, blend the confectioners' sugar with the coffee extract and just enough water to make a thick glaze. Spread a little frosting over each puff. Allow to dry before packing in a rigid container. Chill before transporting.

HALVA YOGURT

SERVES 4-6

3 large cooking apples, peeled, cored and chopped
1 tablespoon lemon juice
1 tablespoon superfine sugar
2 tablespoons butter
2¾ cups thick unflavored yogurt
¼ lb pistachio, almond or vanilla halva (available from delicatessens)
DECORATION
fresh mint sprigs

Place the apples, lemon juice, sugar and butter in a pan. Stir in 1 tablespoon water and cover the pan tightly. Cook very gently for about 10 minutes, shaking the pan frequently until the apples are reduced to a thick pulp. Cool. Stir the apple into the yogurt and finally stir in the halva. Chill and pack into a sealed container or a wide-necked thermos.

DRIED FRUIT COMPÔTE

SERVES 6-8

I cup each dried pears, peaches, apple rings, papaya,
pineapple, figs and apricots (or any preferred
combination), diced
½ cup coffee sugar
5 cups strong hot tea
I teaspoon ground cinnamon
6 tablespoons rum
I cup pitted dates

Mix the dried fruit in a large bowl. Dissolve the
sugar in the tea and add the cinnamon and rum.
Pour the mixture over the fruit and leave to stand
overnight. Pour into a sealed container and
stir in the dates. Chill before packing. Serve with
whipped cream.

SPRING SPECIAL

SERVES 6

2¾ cups fresh orange juice
2 tablespoons grenadine syrup
½ cup Tia Maria liqueur
2¾ cups sparkling mineral water
fresh mint sprigs

Mix the orange juice, grenadine and liqueur in a
thermos. Chill and transport. Just before serving
mix in the mineral water and float mint sprigs on
the surface.

FROSTED CHOCOLATE CAKE

SERVES 8-10

CAKE ROLL
3 eggs
⅓ cup superfine sugar
¾ cup all-purpose flour, sifted
FILLING
1⅓ cups semisweet chocolate, grated
1¼ cups heavy cream
1 tablespoon dark rum
FROSTING
1 cup superfine sugar
6 tablespoons water
pinch cream of tartar
1 egg white

To make the cake roll, beat the eggs and sugar together until very thick, pale and fluffy. Gently fold in the flour and pour the mixture into a greased, lined 9 by 13-inch jelly roll pan. Bake at 400°F for 12 to 15 minutes. Turn out on to sugared waxed paper. Peel off the lining paper and trim the edges. Roll up the sponge with the paper inside. Cool on a wire rack.

To make the filling, place the chocolate, cream and rum in a pan over a gentle heat and stir until blended. Bring briefly to the boil and immediately remove from the heat. Allow to cool until thickened, stirring occasionally. Beat the mixture until thick and fluffy. Unroll the cake, spread with the filling and re-roll.

To make the frosting, place the sugar and water in a small pan and heat gently, stirring, until the sugar dissolves. Add the cream of tartar and bring to the boil. Without stirring, boil until the temperature reaches 240°F on a sugar thermometer (soft ball stage). Meanwhile beat the egg white until stiff. As soon as the syrup has reached the correct temperature remove from the heat and when the bubbles have subsided, pour the syrup in a thin stream on to the egg white while continuing to beat. Beat the mixture until it is very thick (about 3 minutes). Quickly swirl the frosting over the roll. Allow to set.

Pack in a rigid container and serve in slices.

MARBLED CHOCOLATE EGGS

MAKES 6-8

2 cups good quality semisweet chocolate
1 cup white chocolate

Grate the chocolate into separate pitchers. Stand each pitcher in a bowl of hot water and stir until the chocolate melts. (The chocolate should be at 98.4°F when ready to use.) Polish the inside of some small egg-shaped chocolate molds with a clean cloth. Pour the chocolates into a large bowl and very gently stir them together two or three times. Pour the chocolate into the molds to fill and leave them in a cool dry place until the outside layer of chocolate has set to a leathery consistency. Pour or spoon the remaining liquid chocolate out of the egg molds. Trim the edges of the eggs with a knife to make a smooth finish. Allow to stand until completely set.

Gently tap the molds on a surface to release the shapes. Turn out the egg halves. Sandwich the egg halves together in pairs using a little melted chocolate.

To Decorate: The eggs can be decorated with piped lines and loops of icing, or small crystallized fruits or flowers.

POPPY SEED COOKIES

MAKES 25

1½ cups whole wheat flour
⅔ cup medium oatmeal
¼ teaspoon salt
pinch dry mustard
6 tablespoons butter
6 tablespoons milk
1 egg, beaten
3-4 tablespoons poppy seeds

Mix the flour, oatmeal, salt and dry mustard in a bowl. Rub in the butter. Stir in the milk and half the egg and mix to a firm dough. Knead lightly and roll out thinly on a lightly-floured surface. Cut out 3-inch rounds with a cookie cutter. Place on greased baking sheets. Brush with the remaining egg and sprinkle with the poppy seeds. Bake at 400°F for 12 to 15 minutes until golden. Cool on a wire rack. Transport in plastic bags.

WALNUT BREAD

MAKES 2 SMALL LOAVES

½ cake compressed yeast
1¼ cups hand-hot water
4 cups whole wheat flour
1½ teaspoons salt
1 tablespoon butter
3 scallions, chopped
⅓ cup walnuts, chopped
beaten egg, to glaze
sesame seeds

Blend the yeast and water together. Mix the flour and salt in a warmed bowl. Rub in the butter and stir in the onions and nuts. Pour in the yeast liquid and mix to a soft dough. Turn out on to a lightly floured surface and knead until soft and smooth for about 10 minutes. Cut the dough in half and shape each into a roll. Place each in a small greased loaf pan and cover with oiled plastic wrap. Leave to rise in a warm place for about 1 hour until doubled in size. Remove the plastic, brush with beaten egg and sprinkle with seeds. Bake at 450°F for 25 minutes until golden brown and the loaves sound hollow when tapped underneath. Cool on a wire rack.

EASTER BRAID GARLAND

SERVES 8

½ cake compressed yeast
¾ cup lukewarm milk
2 cups all-purpose flour
½ teaspoon salt
2 teaspoons sugar
2 tablespoons butter
FILLING
2 tablespoons butter, melted
¼ cup walnuts, coarsely chopped
¼ cup candied cherries, quartered
½ cup dried apricots, chopped
¼ cup white raisins
¼ cup soft brown sugar
DECORATION
confectioners' sugar

Blend the yeast with the milk. Sift the flour and salt into a large warmed bowl. Stir in the sugar and rub in the butter. Pour in the yeast liquid and mix to a soft dough. Turn out on to a floured surface and knead until smooth and silky. Place in an oiled plastic bag and leave to rise in a warm place until doubled in size. Knock back the risen dough and knead until smooth again. Roll out on a lightly-floured surface to a large rectangle. Brush the dough with the melted butter and scatter the nuts, fruit and sugar over the surface. Roll up the dough from a long side like a jelly roll.

With a sharp knife, cut the roll in half length-ways to make 2 long half-rolls. Press the strips together at one end and then twist them together. Form the twisted dough into a ring and set on a greased baking sheet. Cover with oiled plastic wrap and leave to prove in a warm place for about 20 minutes until puffy.

Remove the plastic and bake the garland at 425°F for about 40 minutes until golden brown. While still hot mix a little sifted confectioners' sugar with enough boiling water to form a thin cream. Brush this glaze over the garland and allow to cool on a wire rack. When cold, wind a ribbon round the garland and tie in a bow to decorate.

Serve in slices.

HOT FRUIT BUNS

MAKES 16

1 cake compressed yeast
1¼ cups hand-hot milk
4 cups all-purpose flour
1 teaspoon salt
2 tablespoons superfine sugar
¼ cup margarine
1½ teaspoons ground mixed spice
¾ cup currants
⅓ cup mixed candied peel
GLAZE
3 tablespoons superfine sugar
7 tablespoons milk

Blend the yeast with the milk. Sift the flour into a bowl with the salt and sugar. Rub in the margarine and stir in the spice. Pour in the yeast liquid and mix to a soft dough. Turn out on to a lightly-floured work surface and knead until soft, smooth and silky. Place in an oiled plastic bag and leave to rise in a warm place until doubled in size.

Knock back the dough and knead in the fruit and peel. Divide the dough into about 16 pieces and roll each into a ball. Place, well spaced on greased baking sheets and cover with oiled plastic wrap. Allow to prove in a warm place for about 40 minutes. Bake at 425°F for 15 to 20 minutes until golden brown.

Meanwhile, place the sugar and milk for the glaze in a small pan. Bring to the boil and simmer for 4 minutes. Brush this glaze over the buns as they come out of the oven. Cool on a wire rack.

Serve split and buttered.

PERFECT PICNIC
TIPS

Even spur-of-the-moment family outings can be turned into perfect picnics. Ready-made vol-au-vent cases can be used with quickly made fillings such as taramasalata, blue cheese and dressed crab beaten to a smooth mixture with cream cheese and seasonings. Or spread celery sticks with a filling, or serve sticks of celery, carrot and cucumber with cups of filling for a dip. Buy croissants, split and fill them with cheese, ham and tomatoes. Sandwich ratafia biscuits together with a little vanilla butter cream for a quick 'dessert'. Spread frosting on the top of pound cake and cut the cake into squares. Top each square with a crystallized violet or rose petal.

KEEPING FOOD HOT
Soups, casseroles and stews can be kept hot in a wide-necked food thermos. For a larger quantity, seal and then wrap a casserole in thick towels or blankets and put the whole into an insulated bag. Alternatively, set the hot container into a large cardboard box filled with straw, cover with straw, then seal the box lid. Keep pies hot in the same way, packed in a cookie tin lined with paper towels to absorb the steam. If there is to be a long period before the food is eaten, it may be more effective to take a small camping burner and reheat the food on arrival.

If you are picnicking on a hike, take very lightweight containers for the food so that they can be carried without discomfort after the meal. Pack squashable foods in foil or use plastic bags. Small, sealable plastic tubs and cups are ideal, light-weight containers. Choose those that fit inside each other when empty so that they take up less space.

Christmas left-overs make excellent picnic foods and this is an ideal way of using up pieces of cooked turkey, ham and beef. Mix cooked meats with raw sliced mushrooms and spiced mayonnaise and serve in pita bread pockets. Spread slices of cooked beef with whole grain mustard or creamed horseradish and roll up to eat with crusty French bread. Christmas cake and fruit pies are good for winter picnics – warm the pies and pack them in a cookie container lined with paper towels.

DRINKS
Plenty of drinks are essential for a perfect picnic, cool and long for summer, steaming hot for cold weather. Tea and coffee are best freshly made on site from a thermos of boiling water or better still, a kettle on a small camping burner. For cold drinks, crushed ice in insulated thermos' or pitchers will help. In very hot weather, freeze the drink completely and it will be ready to drink ice-cold, by the time it's served. Very sweet drinks tend to increase thirst and are better avoided.

Look for unbreakable bottles in plastic or aluminum. Check that the stoppers, lids or seals really do work – even upside down. You don't want a backpack awash with orange juice. Insulated flasks are ideal for hot drinks – look for those with non-breakable inners. Insulated jugs look good but are only suitable for a picnic with transport, as are the large pump-action thermos'. These save you having to lift the thermos' to pour but they are cumbersome.

CHILDREN'S PICNICS
Children love to see their names written on food. Pipe names or initials in frosting on fairy cakes, jello molds and cookies. Use pastry or cookie cutters to stamp initials in sandwiches. Smaller children will especially enjoy an individual party picnic basket. Provide each child with a small basket or box containing a selection of party foods. Tie with ribbon and attach a name label.

AVOIDING BUGS AND SAND
Picnics on summer evenings, whether in the country or on the patio can be spoiled by flying bugs. Light the area with barbecue garden flares, gas lanterns or candles set in glass covers or in jars on poles. Take the precaution of using a special slow-burning light designed to keep mosquitos away, especially near water.

Picnicking on a dry, wind-blown shore can be spoiled if sand gets into the food. Pack foods in lidded containers with deep sides, so that they do not fall over. Set the picnic out on a large clean cloth or towel. Take face towels dipped into cologne-scented water and packed in plastic bags to clean sticky, salty hands and faces. Provide plenty of soft paper towels.

COOLING IT

There is almost nothing worse to eat than a warm tuna mousse so it's a good idea to try and keep picnic foods chilled. A variety of insulated carry boxes are available; some are rigid with fitted lids while others are made of flexible padded plastics with zip closures. The latter have the advantage of folding smaller when empty. Ice packs will help keep the container's inside temperature down and food will stay chilled for several hours.

For an elegant occasion, pack a bag of ice cubes into a wine cooler, and cool the wine thoroughly before leaving home. Wrap the cooled bottles, and put them into the ice cooler immediately you arrive at the picnic site.

GOOD PRESENTATION

For an elegant picnic, there's nothing nicer than china plates, metal cutlery, real napery and glassware for wine and soft drinks. All of these can weigh heavily and need to be very carefully packed.

As an alternative, non-breakable rigid plasticware is available in a variety of patterns and styles, and can also be used for garden entertaining or barbecues. Acrylic tumblers and goblets are lightweight and look almost as good as glass.

WATER COOLER

On a hot day, water can act as a perfect 'refrigerator' for bottled and canned drinks. Stand them securely between rocks in a fast flowing stream or bury them in wet sand at the shore line. Be sure to keep an eye on them though – especially when the tide comes in! At the lake-side, tie unopened bottles and cans into a string bag, submerge it in the water and secure the handles to the bank. When a cool drink is demanded – just haul them in!

CHECK LIST

To ensure a perfect picnic, make a check list of essential items so that nothing is left behind. Don't forget things such as corkscrews, bottle and can openers, a carving knife, salt, pepper and mustard, salad dressings and butter and sharp knives for cutting cheese, slicing cakes and peeling fruit. When packing, plates, cups and cutlery, etc. go in first, then the tablecloth and the rug on top. Then, everything comes out in the right order to spread the picnic.

PLANNING AHEAD
FOR PICNICS

Pre-cooking and freezing will ensure that delicious snacks and sandwiches are readily to hand for spur-of-the-moment excursions, and special dishes for more formal picnics can be planned.

Most foods freeze well but there are a few items which should be avoided.

FOODS UNSUITABLE FOR FREEZING
- Hard-cooked eggs (including eggs in pies, sandwiches, etc.)
- Custards (including pies)
- Soft meringue topping on desserts
- Mayonnaise-type salad dressings
- Milk puddings
- Hard frosting on cakes or cookies
- Salad vegetables
- Stuffed poultry, stuffings
- Foods with a high proportion of gelatin

CHOOSING PACKAGING
Whenever possible, cook foods in containers which can go directly into the freezer. Foods which will need reheating such as casseroles, soups and stews, can be frozen in rigid containers then transferred to ordinary cooking ware for reheating.

Large items, such as whole hams, salmon, terrines, etc. can be wrapped in foil or heavy freezer wrap.

GENERAL GUIDELINES

GALANTINS, MEAT LOAF, ETC. Prepare and cook in loaf pans lined with foil. Freeze in the pan, remove pan from foil for storage.
High Quality Storage Life   2 months
To use, defrost quickly.
Alternatively, freeze in slices with plastic wrap separators. Pack in freezer wrap for freezing.

CRAB AND LOBSTER Cook fresh fish, cool and leave in shell. Wrap in heavy freezer wrap or foil. Alternatively, remove fish from shell, pack into containers, cover and overwrap in freezer wrap or foil.
High Quality Storage Life 1 month
To use, defrost 6-8 hours in the refrigerator.

SOUPS Thicken soups with cornstarch rather than flour when preparing. Seasoning may cause off-flavors, so season after thawing.
Freeze in rigid containers, leaving head space.
High Quality Storage Life 2 months
To use, reheat gently. (Rice, cheese, cream, etc. should be added after heating.)

PASTA DISHES WITH SAUCES Prepare in a freezer dish, cool, cover and freeze.
High Quality Storage Life 2 months
To use, remove the cover, re-cover with foil and heat slowly in the oven.

MOUSSE Prepare and set in freezer container. Cover, then freeze.
High Quality Storage Life 1 month
To use, defrost in the refrigerator for 3-4 hours.

SHORTCRUST PASTRY PIES AND QUICHES
Pastry cases can be frozen raw, or baked and frozen unfilled. For ready-filled cases, prepare and bake as usual, cool, remove from tin and open-freeze. Wrap in foil or freezer wrap, store in a rigid box.
High Quality Storage Life 1 month
To use, defrost at room temperature 3 hours or unwrap and heat in a medium oven for 20 minutes.

CASSEROLES Prepare and cook the dish, transfer to a freezer dish. Cool, cover and freeze.
High Quality Storage Life 2 months
To use, part-defrost, then transfer to an ovenware container. Cover and heat gently for 45 minutes or reheat from frozen in a double pan.

PÂTÉ Prepare in foil containers, cool and cover, freeze.
High Quality Storage Life 1 month
To use, defrost in refrigerator 3 hours.

PERFECT PICNIC MENUS

The menus here are planned to serve parties of varying numbers and the recipes can usually be found within the chapter indicated.

Recipes are not given for foods and accompaniments without page references. These are suggestions to complement the menus.

AT THE WATER'S EDGE

MENU 1   SERVES 6-8

Poached Salmon   page 12
Avocado Swirl   page 11
Mushroom Terrine   page 11
New Potato Salad   page 16
(served with mixed green salad, brown rolls, butter)
Brown Bread Ice Cream   page 17
Brandy Snap Curls   page 17

MENU 2   SERVES 6-8

Chicken Cashew Salad   page 14
Filo Onion Tarts   page 10
Seafood Pasta Salad   page 14
(served with mixed salad, brown rolls, butter)
Rich Chocolate Slice   page 14
(Fresh raspberries and cream)
To drink: Summer Sparkler   page 19

MENU 3   SERVES 6-8

Mushroom Terrine   page 11
Orange Glazed Ham   page 13
Sweet and Sour Carrot Salad   page 15
German Potato Salad   page 15
(served with a tomato and scallion salad)
Creamy Pear and Walnut Pie   page 18
Brandy Snap Curls   page 17

MENU 4   SERVES 6-8

Filo Onion Pies   page 10
Roast Pistachio Chicken   page 18
Omelet Salad   page 16
(served with a green salad and bread sticks)
Fragrant Honey Mousse   page 19
Rich Chocolate Slice   page 18
(a selection of seasonal fruit)

A WALK IN THE COUNTRY

MENU 1   SERVES 6

Pork and Cranberry Samosas   page 23
Garlic Tortilla Omelet in Pita Bread   page 26
Vegetable Sticks and Blue Cheese Dip   page 80
Apple and Almond Danish Pastries   page 29
Choc Nut Rocks   page 30
To drink: Homemade Lemonade   page 31
(fresh fruit)

MENU 2   SERVES 6

Peppery Chicken Turnovers   page 27
Spiced Meat Balls and Dip   page 26
Potted Stilton and crackers   page 22
(plus a coleslaw salad)
Gingered Almond Loaf   page 29
Apricot Brandy Cream Mousse   page 28

MENU 3   SERVES 6

Hearty Bean Soup   page 25
Sagey Pork Turnovers   page 22
Taramasalata and Pita bread   page 22
Creamy Mushroom Puffs   page 23
Apricot and Walnut Slice   page 29
Flaky Cheese and Apple Strudel   page 28

MENU 4   SERVES 6

Potted Danish Blue   page 22
Chicken and Veal Terrine   page 25
(whole wheat rolls and butter)
Fresh Tomato Chutney   page 24
Fruited Flapjack   page 30
Apple and Almond Danish Pastries   page 29

SUMMER INTERLUDE

MENU 1   SERVES 6-8

Shrimp and Asparagus Mousse   page 35
(served with a celery and corn salad)
Mushroom Pie   page 35
Creamy Apple and Horseradish Chicken
page 37
Mixed Wild Rice Salad   page 38
Rosemary Bread Sticks   page 42
Japonaise Fingers   page 43
Kiwi Citrus Fruit Salad and cream   Page 40

MENU 2   SERVES 6-8

Raised Chicken and Ham Pie   page 37
Tricolor Vegetable Terrine   page 34
Greek Salad   page 39
Saffron Bread   page 42
Cassata   page 40
Florentines   page 43
(a selection of fresh fruit)

MENU 3   SERVES 6

Mozzarella and Tomato Salad   page 39
Rosemary Bread Sticks   page 42
Salad Niçoise   page 38
Salmon and Lemon Terrine   page 36
(serve with crusty bread, new potatoes, coleslaw and
a salad)
Poached Pears   page 41
Florentines   page 43
(a selection of cheeses)

MENU 4   SERVES 6

Seafood Cocktails   page 34
Olive and Anchovy Bread   page 42
Mixed Wild Rice Salad   page 38
(plus a coleslaw and a green salad)
Dark and White Chocolate Mousse   page 41
Japonaise Cakes   page 43

CHILDREN'S PICNICS

For birthday picnics, each menu to be supplemented
by a birthday cake of your choice

MENU 1   SERVES 8-10

Barbecue Chicken Chunks   page 46
Cheesy Cookies   page 46
Sesame Puff Fingers   page 49
Egg and Cress Mini Loaves   page 50
(crisps, savory nibbles)
Strawberry Cup Cakes   page 52
Lemon Meringue Ice Cream   page 54
To drink: fizzy bottled drinks or fruit juice

MENU 2   SERVES 8-10

Sausage Twirls   page 47
Buttered Cheese Bagels   page 47
Savory Tomato Butterflies   page 48
Eggy Buns   page 48
Caramel Fingers   page 53
Lime and Strawberry Jelly Mousse   page 53

MENU 3   SERVES 8-10

Egg and Cress Mini Loaves   page 50
Cheese, Fruit and Nut Nibbles   page 50
Cheese and Celery Nut Bread   page 51
Mini Bacon Pies   page 49
(crisps, celery and carrot sticks)
Chocolate Boxes   page 52

MENU 4   SERVES 8-10

Buttered Cheese Bagels   page 47
Barbecue Chicken Chunks   page 46
Herby Sausages with Mustard Dip   page 51
(crisps, savory nibbles)
Lemon Cup Cakes   page 52
Caramel Fingers   page 53
Fresh Lemon and Lime Punch   page 54

FOOD FOR LOVE

MENU 1   SERVES 2

Spicy Potted Shrimp   page 58
Herbed French Stick with Garlic Butter
page 65
Tortellini and Sour Cream Salad   page 73
Cress and Palm Heart Salad   page 74
Frosting-dipped Fruits   page 63
Orange and Rosewater Bavarois   page 62

MENU 2   SERVES 2

Blue Cheese, Bacon and Apple Salad   page 74
(whole wheat pita bread)
Pork Satay   page 67
(Cucumber salad)
Chicken Tikka Pieces   page 60
Crab and Chicken Roll   page 60
Creamy Dutch Syllabub   page 64
Sponge Drops   page 63
(a selection of fresh fruit)

MENU 1   SERVES 8-10

Celery, Ham and Carrot Salad   page 72
Chicken Galantine   page 71
Cold Parslied Ratatouille Salad   page 72
Herbed French Stick with butter   page 65 (make
recipe × 3)
Cœur à la Crème   page 75
Frosting-dipped Fruits   page 63 (make
recipe × 4)

MENU 2   SERVES 6

Pork Satay   page 67 (make recipe × 3)
Savory Stilton Milles Feuilles   page 68
Tortellini and Sour Cream Salad   page 73
Mushroom Brioche   page 67
(green salad)
Special Summer Pudding   page 75
Sponge Fingers   page 63 (make recipe × 3)
(a selection of cheeses)

FALL BOUNTY

MENU 1   SERVES 8-10

Creamy Ham Croustades   page 79
Smoked Trout Baklava   page 78
Almond-filled Meringues   page 85
Crunchy Caramel Cones   page 86
Open Cherry Pies   page 84
Coffee Brazil Snaps   page 84

MENU 2   SERVES 8-10

Ham and Cheese Croissants   page 79
Ricotta and Smoked Salmon Turnovers
page 81
Vegetable Crudités with Garlic and Walnut
Dip   page 80
(brown bread and butter)
Frangipane Pie   page 82
White Raisin Streusel Cake   page 87
Paris Brest Gâteau   page 84

MENU 3   SERVES 6-8

Potted Tongue and crackers   page 78
Cheese and Mustard Cups   page 79
Vegetable Crudités with Green Herb Dip   page 80
Baked Plum Cheesecake   page 87
Raspberry Pies   page 84
To drink: Creamed Chocolate Drink   page 88

MENU 4   SERVES 6-8

Pine Nut Savory Bread   page 83
Veal and Tongue Terrine   page 80
(water cress and celery)
Honey and White Raisin Biscuits   82
Rose Petal Jelly   page 88
(bread and butter)
Chocolate Croissants   page 79
Paris Brest Gâteau   page 84

NEW YEARS DAY

MENU 1   SERVES 6-8

Tomato Chowder   page 93
(whole wheat rolls and butter)
Mustard Ham in Pastry   page 94
Peppered Roast Beef   page 96
Pink Grapefruit and Avocado Salad   page 98
(serve with mixed salad and mixed pickles)
Stollen   page 101
Orange and Almond Fruit Pies with
Cointreau Butter   page 99

MENU 2   SERVES 6-8

Pink Grapefruit and Avocado Salad   page 98
Cassoulet Pot   page 92
(baked jacket potatoes)
French Beans Vinaigrette   page 98
Rum Babas   page 100
Snowy Chocolate Truffles   page 100
To drink: Hot Spiced Mull   page 103

MENU 3   SERVES 6-8

Chicken Noodle Soup   page 93
Beef Pastry Turnovers   page 96
(serve with a mixed salad and a coleslaw salad)
Caramel Almond Pie   page 101
Stollen   page 101
To drink: Honey Glogg   page 102

MENU 4   SERVES 6-8

Creamy Pesto Tagliatelle Salad   page 97
Nutty Bacon Braid   page 95
French Beans Vinaigrette   page 98
Cocktail Tandoori Chicken   page 95
(celery and a cream, or blue-veined, cheese)
Orange and Almond Fruit Pies and
Brandied Cream   page 99
To drink: Cider Glow   page 102

SPRING EXCURSION

MENU 1   SERVES 4-6

Brandied Liver Pâté   page 106
Poppy Seed Cookies   page 115
(served with celery)
Rich Beef and Beet Hotpot   page 110
Mushroom and Parsley Pilau   page 108
Easter Braid Garland   page 116
Marbled Chocolate Eggs   page 114

MENU 2   SERVES 4-6

Chili Shrimp and Avocado Cream   page 107
Puff Top Chicken and Walnut Pies   page 109
Potato Chestnut Casserole   page 111
(French stick and butter)
Halva Yogurt   page 112
Frosted Chocolate Cake   page 114
(served with whipped cream)
To drink: Spring Special   page 113

MENU 3   SERVES 4-6

Tropical Lentil Soup   page 108
Orchard Pork Casserole   page 110
Mushroom Rice Salad   page 108
Coffee Choux Puffs   page 112
Hot Fruit Buns   page 116
Poppy Seed Cookies   page 115
(a selection of cheeses)

MENU 4   SERVES 6-8

Brandied Liver Pâté   page 116
(served with celery sticks)
Walnut Bread   page 115
Chili Shrimp and Avocado Cream   page 107
Bacon and Pine Nut Filo Wheels   page 107
(serve with a mixed salad and a coleslaw salad)
Dried Fruit Compôte   page 113
Halva Yogurt   page 112
To drink: Spring Special   page 113

INDEX